Beginner's Guide to
TRADITIONAL ARCHERY

Brian J. Sorrells

STACKPOLE
BOOKS

Published by
STACKPOLE BOOKS
5067 Ritter Road
Mechanicsburg, PA 17055
www.stackpolebooks.com

Printed in the United States of America

10 9 8 7 6 5 4 3

Cover design by Caroline Stover

Photographs by Bill Phillips

Library of Congress Cataloging-in-Publication Data

Sorrells, Brian J.
    Beginner's guide to traditional archery / Brian J. Sorrells.— 1st ed.
      p. cm.
    Includes bibliographical references and index.
    ISBN 0-8117-3133-2
    1. Bowhunting. 2. Archery. I. Title.
SK36.S66 2004
799.2'028'5—dc22

                                    2004003337

    ISBN 978-0-8117-3133-1

DISCLAIMER

Safety is the ultimate concern any time an individual is engaged in activities with potential for serious injury. Traditional archery is no different. This book is written as an instructional manual, and all possible precautions should be taken to safely engage in the activities outlined herein. The author assumes no responsibility for any injury, loss, or inconvenience sustained by any person using this book. It is the sole responsibility of the reader to ensure that the shooting area is safe, that the reader's archery equipment is in proper working order, and that the reader has no health problems that may interfere with or be aggravated by engaging in the activities described in this book.

Contents

Acknowledgments

I would like to thank all those who have helped in this endeavor, either directly or indirectly.

Thanks the most to my dad, Bill Sorrells (August 17, 1925–October 1, 1999), who instilled in me a love of hunting and the outdoors that only keeps growing, a love that I will pass on to my two daughters, Rachel and Claire.

Thanks to my family for giving me enough time in front of the computer to complete this project, even though I could, and probably should, have been doing other things. Thanks to T. J. Conrads and Don Thomas at *Traditional Bowhunter* and Dwight Schuh at *Bowhunter* for the enormous help and opportunities they have given me.

A very special and heartfelt thanks to Bill Phillips, a.k.a. the Computer Guru, for his infinite wisdom and assistance in putting the book together. Not only a computer whiz, his photography and videography deserve a round of applause, also! Without Bill, this book would be just a bunch of words on a floppy disk! Another special thanks to Janet Phillips, former schoolteacher, who helped with my punctuation problems.

Thank you to Keith Chastain, master bowyer and owner of Wapiti Bows, for his helpful advice on choosing a bowyer. Thanks also to all the other hardworking bowyers out there who produce beautiful bows.

Thanks to my hunting partner and fellow police officer, Danny Phillips. I truly enjoy your company on those early morning rides to our hunting spots, as well as your taste in music.

And to everyone else who has had a positive impact on my life, thank you.

Introduction

The bow and arrow, in various forms, have been around for thousands of years. The advent of the compound bow a few decades ago allowed the archer to shoot a swifter, flatter-flying arrow. Along came sight pins and range finders to give the archer an extra advantage in the field. But more and more compound bow shooters are discovering that those advances in archery technology are accompanied by the headaches of more required maintenance and a higher occurrence of mechanical failure in the field.

I believe that's one of the reasons for the resurgence of interest in traditional archery and instinctive shooting. Not only is the equipment much simpler, but also the challenge for the archer is greater. A traditional bow does not require a special press or tool to change a bowstring. The arrow rest usually consists of a simple piece of leather or rug that requires no fine-tuning. There are no sight pins to come loose or break off, leaving the shooter helpless at the moment of truth.

Nearly every person has the natural ability within him or her to shoot a bow and arrow instinctively. Instinctive shooting is shooting a bow without the aid of any type of mechanical sight. Much like a pitcher throwing a baseball, the archer uses his or her mind and muscle memory to cause the arrow to hit the target by "feeling" when the shot is lined up correctly instead of relying on mechanical sights to line the bow up for him or her. This "feeling," or sight picture, is gained only through repetition and experience with shooting the bow at different distances. It's just a matter of harnessing this instinct and guiding it through a structured program that will assist the archer in developing that natural ability to its fullest potential. This book is intended to do just that.

Many years ago, when I bought my first recurve bow during the beginning of the compound bow craze, I didn't know any traditional archers, and knew only one instinctive compound shooter, and had no one to show me how to shoot instinctively. The proprietor of the archery shop where I bought the recurve didn't offer much advice either, except to tell me to "stick the pop top off of a soda can on the target, and shoot at the hole until you can hit it every time." Right idea, wrong application. The methods and ideas in the book are based on the simple principle of building a foundation. Each new step depends upon the successful completion of the previous step to make it work. It is important to follow the program as it is written to achieve the desired results.

My hope is that this book will help those of you who are seeking to shoot traditional bows instinctively to be successful and to reach your potential. I strongly recommend that you read this entire book at least once before beginning your instinctive shooting program. It may save you time and money on equipment selection and help you make the choices that are right for you.

- 1 -

Perfect Practice Makes Perfect

Just a little pep talk before we start. Learning to shoot a traditional bow instinctively requires hard work, dedication, and lots of patience. There are no shortcuts to becoming a proficient instinctive shooter, and there are no timetables or schedules to follow. This program relies on repetitive practice using correct shooting form to build muscle memory and hand-eye coordination that will be stored in your brain. This information will be called up each time you shoot an arrow, and your brain and body will use the stored information to perform the task correctly. If you don't practice correctly, you can't learn to be a good instinctive shooter.

Actions performed repeatedly become a habit. If these actions are repeated in the correct manner, the result is a good, useful habit. The most important thing you need to remember in the beginning is to use correct shooting form. By doing so, you will build a solid foundation for your shooting style that will enable you to achieve positive results with your instinctive shooting program. If you try to cheat, shortcut the program, or jump ahead because you're impatient to learn faster, you'll only be hurting yourself. You'll notice as you go through the chapters that some are broken down into steps. Each step in the foundation-building process needs to be completed before moving on to the next one, and each should be completed at your own pace. It's just like building a house—you start from the ground up.

If you get tired while shooting, stop and rest for a while. Fatigue breeds inefficiency, and inefficiency in your shooting form may develop into a bad habit that you will have to go back and correct later on. If you're too tired to come to full draw, then you may do what is known

Shooting while fatigued can lead to bad habits like "short drawing" the bow—not coming to full draw before releasing the arrow.

as "short drawing" the bow. This results in poor arrow flight and errant shots, and fails to make use of the bow's power. Or you may "snap shoot" the arrow because subconsciously your mind is telling your body that it's too tired to hold the string back any longer.

If you get frustrated while shooting, for whatever reason, then quit and come back when you have a positive mental attitude again. Frustration leads to anger, which disrupts the learning process and clouds your judgment. A positive mental attitude has as much to do with your success as an instinctive shooter as does proper equipment. It's better to shoot one arrow with perfect form and control than to shoot 100 arrows with less-than-perfect form.

You need to set aside time to practice, every day if you can, in a place that is as free from outside distractions as possible. Instinctive shooting requires intense concentration, especially in the beginning, and it's hard to concentrate with a lot going on around you. If you don't have a place to shoot at home, see if you have an obliging neighbor with a safe area where you can put up a target and practice your instinctive shooting skills. Another alternative is a local archery range or shop. See if the owner will allow you to set aside a time to shoot by yourself. There's always less pressure to perform when nobody is standing there watching you, and you can concentrate on your shooting form instead of what's going on around you. While it's important to shoot as often as you can, the quality of your repetitive shooting form is more important than the number of arrows shot. Continue shooting only as long as you can maintain concentration and correct shooting form.

Set goals for yourself, but be realistic. Avoid the pitfalls of fatigue and frustration. Remember, this is a learning process and must be done at your own pace. Some individuals learn quickly because they possess greater natural skills and athletic ability, and others because they have a great deal of drive and enthusiasm.

How far you go and how well you do with your instinctive shooting will be entirely dependent upon your hard work, dedication, and positive mental attitude. Instinctive shooting is like most other things in life: you get out of it what you put into it.

- 2 -

The Right Equipment

Just like any other activity, instinctive shooting requires that you have the right tools for the job. In order for you to perform at your optimum level, all pieces of your equipment must be matched to each other and to you. If you're just starting out with traditional archery and instinctive shooting, it's easier to decide what your needs and preferences are and then go out and buy equipment than it is to take what gear you might already have and try to make it work. That's one of the great things about traditional archery as a shooting sport: with a modest initial investment, you can keep shooting as long as you want without having to go out and buy more ammunition. Unless, of course, you bend, break, or lose all of your arrows. You will need the following equipment for the exercises outlined in this book:

1. The traditional bow of your choice in a suitable draw weight and bow length, and a good-quality bowstringer.
2. A set of arrows that are of the proper spine and length to shoot from your bow at your draw weight.
3. A shooting tab or glove and an armguard. Though the armguard is optional, it may save you a painful bruise if the bowstring should slap your forearm.
4. A quality bag-type archery target of the biggest size you can afford. If you have a used one, make sure it's in good condition, with no hard spots that would cause an arrow to bounce back and no thin spots that an arrow will pass through.
5. As important as anything else, *a safe place to shoot!*

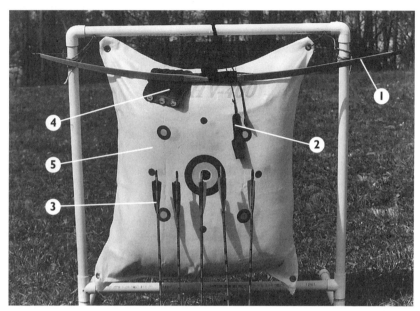

Traditional archery is a simple sport and requires only a modest investment in equipment. Pictured here are 1) a traditional bow, 2) a bowstringer, 3) arrows, 4) an armguard, and 5) a bag target.

THE BOW

The most basic and necessary piece of equipment is the bow. There are many styles of traditional bows today. Recurves, longbows, Indian-style flatbows, and selfbows all have their following, and all have something to offer the shooter who wants a simpler way to shoot. Traditional bows vary widely in quality and price, from the mass-produced bows made by well-known archery manufacturers and suppliers to the handmade custom bows produced one at a time by the skilled hands of a custom bowyer.

Selecting a Bow

Make sure that the bow style you choose is what you want. Longbows and recurve bows are the most common styles of traditional bows seen in the hands of shooters today. The recurve bow is easily identified by the ends of the bow limbs, which curve away from the shooter. Longbows have thicker, narrower limbs with little or no curve. Each has its

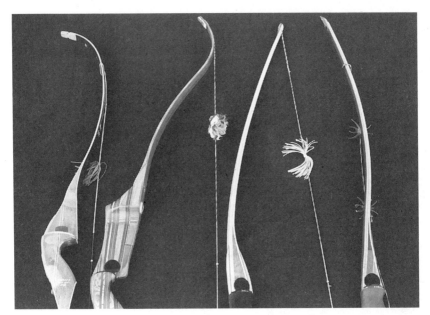

Recurves (left) and longbows (right) are the two most common bow styles in use today.

own attributes, and I own both styles. While a recurve is known more for its arrow speed, a longbow is best for shooting a heavy shaft with a lot of authority. The choice is up to you. Before choosing a bow, make sure you handle and draw as many as you can. One bow may feel better in your hand than another.

Differences in grip styles and the physical weight of the bow can help make your decision easier also. There are generally three different grip styles you'll see. A high wrist grip places the pressure of the grip in the web of the hand because the hand points down, causing the wrist to come up, hence the name. A low wrist grip places the pressure from the bow's grip closer to the heel of the hand; the bones in the wrist and forearm are more in alignment, allowing the pressure of drawing the bow to be distributed more evenly through the joints. A medium wrist grip falls somewhere between the two, with varying degrees of angle on different bows. Grip is a matter of personal taste. That's why I strongly urge you to shop around, and look at and handle as many bows as you can, before choosing one to take home with you.

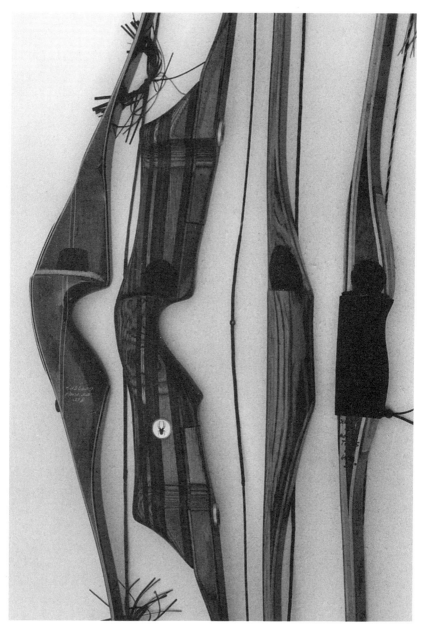

Bows come with grips in different styles. The shape of the grip should be comfortable in your hand in order to shoot the bow accurately.

I will, however, give you important advice on draw weight and bow length. Draw weight is more important than any other factor when choosing your bow. The leading cause of shooters giving up traditional archery prematurely is that they try to shoot a bow with too much draw weight. Don't fall into the trap of thinking that you have to shoot a traditional bow pulling 65 to 75 pounds to get any arrow speed. With the materials and technology used in the manufacturing of today's traditional bows, most of them shoot at a speed equal to or greater than the speed of the original wheeled compound bow. Besides, accuracy is infinitely more important than arrow speed in instinctive shooting. Starting out, 35 to 45 pounds of draw weight is plenty. If you have any question about whether a draw weight is too much for you, try this: Pick up the bow, hold it out in front of you, and try to draw the bowstring straight back to the corner of your mouth. If you have to point the bow up or down, or go through some wild gyrations to get the bowstring back, then that's too much draw weight. You should be able to draw the bow comfortably and smoothly straight back to anchor, and to do this repeatedly.

Bow length is another factor to consider. While traditional bows come in a wide variety of lengths, your physical stature and draw length will help determine what length of bow is right for you. For example, if you're 6 feet, 6 inches tall with a 30-inch draw length, you probably shouldn't be shooting a little 52-inch recurve bow. At your draw length, a bow that short would cause a severe angle in the bowstring, pinching the fingers of the drawing hand. A more suitable bow would be a longbow or recurve in the 64- to 68-inch range, which would provide a less severe string angle and make for a smoother draw. On the other hand, if you're 4 feet, 6 inches tall, it would probably be a little awkward for you to try to shoot a 68-inch longbow. Common sense goes a long way when considering bow length.

While I don't recommend starting out with an $800 custom bow if you're just learning instinctive shooting, I certainly don't recommend starting out with a $10 pawn shop special, either. Get yourself a good bow made by one of the well-known bow-manufacturing companies such as Bear Archery, Martin Archery, or PSE. Then, later, as you gain skill and experience, you can invest in a custom-made bow if you choose to.

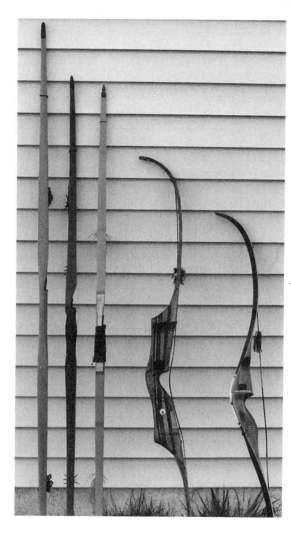

Traditional bows come in sizes to fit any archer.

One option you might want to consider is a takedown bow. On takedown bows, the limbs are bolted to the riser and easily removed when not in use. As your strength increases, you can purchase increasingly heavier sets of limbs to fit on the riser, and save yourself the cost of a new bow with a heavier draw weight. Takedown bows are also nice when traveling, as they can be disassembled and placed in a case, not requiring much room. Once you arrive at your shooting destination, you can reassemble the bow and be ready to shoot.

*Takedown bows
are handy for
traveling and can
fit in a suitcase
or duffel bag.*

Most traditional archers shoot "off the shelf," which means there is no conventional arrow rest as on a compound bow. This is a simple and very reliable method that requires a shelf rest and strike plate to be applied to the arrow shelf and the bow's riser. Most archery shops and mail order catalogs offer commercially made shelf rest and strike plate materials, but simple Velcro works just fine, using the fuzzy pile side, not the stiff loop side. Adhesive-backed Velcro is available in pieces large enough to be cut to fit any bow. Leather can also be cut to fit the bow and glued on using a quality rubber cement. The use of rubber cement reduces the chance of damage to the bow's finish should you need to

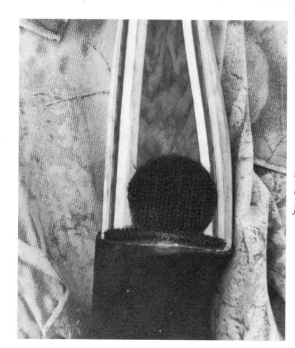

The shelf rest and strike plate provide a launching pad for the arrow.

replace the shelf rest or strike plate. The shelf rest, which is applied to the bow's arrow shelf, serves as a platform or launch pad for the arrow and to quiet the noise of the arrow being drawn. The strike plate, which goes on the bow's riser immediately next to the arrow shelf, serves the same purpose. The shelf rest can be cut to cover the entire arrow shelf, but only needs to be big enough to cover the area where a nocked arrow rests. The strike plate can be as wide as you want it to be, but only needs to come up high enough to cover the sweep of the feathers as they pass across the riser. Whatever material you choose, make sure it allows the arrow to pass smoothly and silently across the shelf and riser.

Ultimately, the choice of bow style is up to you. Shop around, compare, and get something you'll be happy with. If you already have a bow, be sure it's one you're comfortable with. Don't try to go through this program being "overbowed."

Bowstrings

Your bow is designed to work proficiently at a certain brace height. The brace height is the distance from the bowstring to the innermost part of

The brace height is the distance from the bowstring to the innermost part of the grip when the bow is braced, or strung.

the grip and is determined by the length of the bowstring. This measurement is taken while the bow is strung but not drawn. A lower brace height, where the string is closer to the bow, will allow more power stroke from the bow limbs and give slightly more energy to the bow. However, a lower brace height can also make the bow a little less forgiving of a poor release. A higher brace height can make the bow more forgiving but robs the bow limbs of some of their potential energy because the power stroke is shorter.

Most bowmakers give a range of acceptable brace heights for their bows. For example, Bows Inc. recommends that the brace height for their "X" model recurve should be between 7 and 8 inches. Shooting the bow at a brace height outside the manufacturer's recommendation not only robs the bow of power, but also may void the warranty if damage occurs. Consult the owner's manual to find the recommended brace height; if you don't have an owner's manual, write the company and ask for one. Brace heights vary among different styles and makers of bows. Since the brace height is determined by string length, it must be

Wax your bowstring every time you shoot your bow.

adjusted by lengthening or shortening the string. Keep in mind that all new bowstrings will stretch as they are breaking in, so be sure to follow the bowmaker's instructions for adjusting the brace height. This usually involves adding twist to the bowstring. Wax your bowstring with a quality string wax on a regular basis to lengthen the life of the bow- string. Always inspect the bowstring for wear or broken strands before shooting, and replace a damaged bowstring immediately. When order- ing or purchasing a new bowstring, order the string according to the AMO limb length, which is the industry standard for string length. A good rule to remember is that a bowstring that is too long can be made shorter by twisting it, but a string that is too short to start with may not stretch enough to bring the brace height within the manufacturer's requirements.

When stringing and unstringing your bow, use a quality bow- stringer. This will help prevent damage to the bow and injury to you. Some bowmakers will not honor their warranty if they discover that a bowstringer was not used during the stringing or unstringing process

Using a bowstringer is the easiest and safest way to string and unstring your bow.

and damage resulted to the bow. For that reason, most bow companies provide a stringer with the bow. If you don't have one, get one, and learn how to use it. It will save you trouble in the future.

You'll also want to consider purchasing a string silencer. Most traditional bows are inherently quiet to begin with. But just like a plucked guitar string, traditional bows will produce an audible vibration after the shot if some type of silencer is not used. This vibration is caused by excess energy from the bow limbs that was not absorbed by the arrow. The noise can range from a low hum to a resonant ringing sound, depending upon how much energy was left in the bow after the shot. If you're a target shooter, the noise poses no problems. But if you're a bowhunter, that noise can alert an already wary game animal that something is wrong. No bow in the world can shoot an arrow faster than the speed of sound. The result could be the animal "jumping the string," causing a complete miss or, worse yet, a hit in a nonvital area, resulting in a long tracking job and the possibility of not recovering the wounded animal.

The goal is to turn that hum into a dull thump that isn't loud enough to spook an animal. The majority of bow noise can be eliminated simply by shooting a heavier arrow. Between 8 and 11 grains of arrow weight per pound of draw weight is a good rule of thumb. Whatever noise is left over can usually be taken care of with string silencers.

There are many different types of string silencers on the market, with the simplest being the cat whisker type. Cat whiskers consist of a strip of thin rubber that has been scored to allow the strip to separate into tiny filaments. Most archers simply put the silencer on and allow the vibration of the bow to separate the strip into filaments. Cat whiskers can be tied directly to the bowstring or tied onto the bowstring with serving material. Another method is to separate the bowstring into equal halves, insert the section of cat whisker between the halves, then tie it in place with serving material or dental floss.

Another type of string silencer is the puff type. Puff silencers can be made of yarn, beaver fur, polar fleece, or my favorite, sheep's wool.

Pictured left to right: puff-type silencer made from natural wool, cat whiskers made from scored rubber, and spider-shaped silencers made from unscored rubber.

Most puff-type silencers are designed to be inserted between strands of the bowstring and do an excellent job of quieting the bow.

The string silencers should be placed on the bowstring at an equal distance from each limb tip in order to preserve the dynamic balance of the bow limbs. You have to play with the location, moving the string silencers up or down the bowstring to find where they provide the greatest harmonic dampening effect.

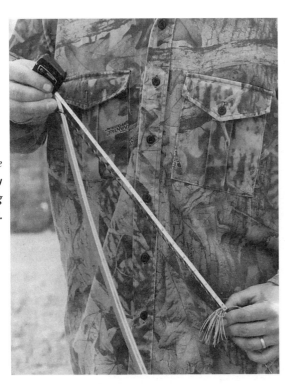

Make sure the silencers are evenly spaced on the bowstring to maintain balance.

Too many or the wrong type of string silencers can add weight to the bowstring and slow it down, which in turn slows down the arrow. Though this amount of performance loss is minimal, avoid using more string silencers than necessary to achieve a noise level that is satisfactory to you. Cat whiskers are heavier than the puff-type string silencers and cause more performance loss. Puff-type silencers, on the other hand, have a greater tendency to collect weed seeds and moisture. Experiment with different types to see what works best for you.

ARROWS

Some traditional shooters look at the arrow as the most important part of the archery equation, even going so far as to say that the bow is nothing more than a launch pad for the arrow. This is partially true. Imagine trying to fire a section of a tree branch from an $800 custom bow. Nothing good is likely to come out of that. The branch isn't spined correctly for the bow and definitely won't be as straight as it should be. The result? Poor arrow flight. Now, say you take that same section of tree branch and make a bow out of it by attaching a piece of string. With this crude, ugly little bow, you shoot a properly spined and finished arrow with the proper weight field point and feather fletching. The arrow will fly like a dart from the primitive bow. That's a rather extreme example, but you get the point. A properly spined arrow combined with feather fletching and a field point of the correct weight will allow your bow to achieve optimum performance.

Each bow should come with an owner's manual that will cover important topics like recommended arrow weight, warranty information, and what type of bowstring to use. If you don't have an owner's

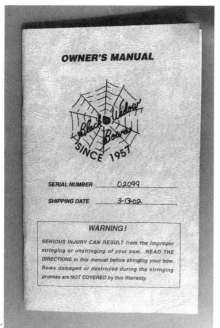

The owner's manual contains vital information for your bow, covering not only tuning and maintenance but also warranty information.

manual for your bow, contact the manufacturer, tell them what type of bow you have, and ask for an owner's manual. Most manufacturers are happy to send one out so that the customer is fully aware of the warranty and its limitations.

Selecting Arrows

Before choosing your arrow shaft, you must know two things: your draw length and the draw weight of your bow at your draw length. Determining draw length is a simple matter. The easiest way is to visit your local archery shop and ask to have your draw length measured using a draw check bow. A draw check bow is simply a fiberglass bow of very light draw weight with an arrow permanently attached to the string. The arrow is marked in quarter-inch increments. Draw the bow back, anchor the string at the corner of your mouth, and have someone read the measurement on the arrow at the point where the arrow passes over the far side of the arrow shelf (the side farthest away from you). This is your draw length. Another method is to use a traditional bow with a light draw weight that allows you to come to full draw and hold

Mark the arrow where it crosses the far side of the arrow shelf.

at anchor without strain. Put an arrow on the string, and with the bow pointed in a safe direction, come to full draw and anchor. Have someone make a mark on the arrow at the point where it crosses the far side of the arrow shelf. Then measure the length from the bottom of the nock groove to the mark on the shaft. This will be your draw length.

Once you've determined your draw length, you will know how much weight you are drawing with your bow. Most traditional bows are marked with the draw weight, which is measured at 28 inches of draw. This information will probably appear on the bow as, for example, 50#@28". What this says is that the bow in the example has a draw weight of 50 pounds when the string is drawn to 28 inches. On most

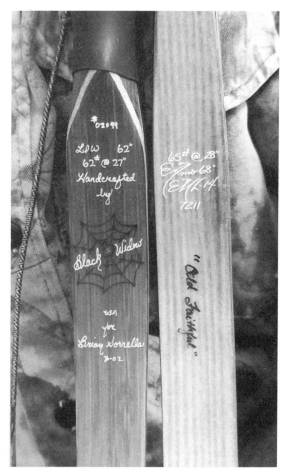

On most traditional bows, the draw length is measured at 28 inches. On the custom bow on the left, the draw weight was measured at 27 inches, the archer's draw length.

quality bows, the draw weight will either increase or decrease by 2 to 3 pounds with each inch of draw over or under 28 inches. For example, if your bow is marked 50 pounds at 28 inches and your draw length is only 27 inches, then you are actually only drawing between 47 and 48 pounds. If, however, your draw length is 29 inches, then you would actually be pulling 52 or 53 pounds. The best way to tell for sure is to take your bow to an archery shop and have it put on a bow scale. Have the bowstring drawn to your draw length, and read the amount of weight shown on the bow scale. I've found in the past that on some mass-produced traditional bows, the draw weight marked on the bow is not the true draw weight. On some bows I've owned, the difference has been as much as 6 or 7 pounds. If there is any doubt, put the bow on a scale, because knowing how much weight you're drawing is vitally important for choosing the arrow shaft of the correct spine ("spine" refers to an arrow's stiffness). On custom-made bows, the draw weight can be made to your personal draw length. The length of the bow from tip to tip is normally written in the same location as the draw weight.

Once you know your draw length and the draw weight of your bow at your draw length, you can choose what type of arrow shaft material you want to shoot. The most common arrow shaft materials are carbon, aluminum, and various types of wood, with aluminum probably being the most popular. Each type has its good and bad points. You don't have to worry about bending carbon shafts, and it takes a lot to break them. One drawback is the fact that carbon shafts

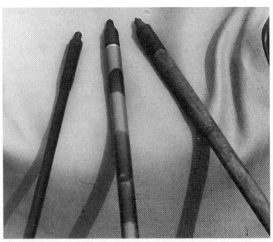

From left to right: carbon, aluminum, and wood shafts.

Wood shafts must be tapered on each end to accept a nock and field point or broadhead. Tapering tools will automatically cut the correct angle for each.

are generally too light to shoot from a traditional bow without adding some weight to the finished shaft. And, if you happen to lose a carbon arrow while shooting, you've lost a fairly expensive item. Aluminum shafts are relatively inexpensive compared with carbon, but they have a tendency to bend easily. Only a few people have the patience and know-how to straighten a bent shaft enough to make it worth shooting again. Wood shafts are the least expensive of the three types but require the most work. Each end of the shaft must be carefully tapered to accept the nock and field point or broadhead. The shaft must also be sealed to prevent moisture from entering and causing it to warp. Unless you buy a set of raw wood shafts that have been matched in spine and weight, which brings the cost up around that of aluminum, the shafts you purchase may differ widely from each other. That will cause each finished arrow from that set of raw shafts to have different shooting characteristics. Of course, you can always purchase a set of finished wood arrows that have been closely matched in spine and weight, but the cost is more than most shooters are willing to pay, especially if an archer shoots a lot and loses or breaks a few arrows occasionally. The choice is up to you. While I know several traditional shooters who lovingly handcraft their own wood arrows and won't shoot anything else, I prefer to shoot aluminum arrows. To me, aluminum is the best choice with the fewest drawbacks.

To find carbon and aluminum arrows that are correct for your bow, you need to consult a spine chart. Major arrow manufacturers and some custom bowmakers publish spine charts to help shooters decide which shaft sizes will perform best from their bows. Most archery shops have spine charts for both carbon and aluminum arrows. Also, most mail-order catalogs that offer arrows show a spine chart on the pages where the arrows are displayed.

To use the spine chart, you'll need to know the draw weight of the bow (remember, use how much weight *you* are drawing, not how much the bow is marked for at 28 inches) and the correct arrow length. Your correct arrow length will be your draw length plus $1\frac{1}{2}$ inches. The extra $1\frac{1}{2}$ inches is to make sure that the field point or broadhead doesn't get dangerously close to either your hand or the bow should you overdraw slightly. For example, if your draw length is 29 inches, your arrow length should finish out no less than $30\frac{1}{2}$ inches. You'll need full-length shafts for bare shaft tuning, so don't worry about getting any shafts cut to length just yet. You just need to know what the finished shaft length will be to use the spine chart.

When choosing an arrow, you must also pay attention to the finished weight—how much the arrow weighs when the nock, fletching, insert, and field point or broadhead have been added. Arrow weight is measured in grains, and there are 437.5 grains in 1 ounce. Every archery shop should have at least one scale that measures weight accurately in grains. These scales are invaluable when it comes to the finer points of arrow building and matching your arrow components by weight.

Every manufacturer of traditional bows has a recommended "grains of arrow weight per pound of draw weight" minimum for their bows. Usually this is between 6 and 8 grains. For example, if the draw weight of the bow is 50 pounds and the manufacturer recommends at least 6 grains of arrow weight per pound of draw weight, then your finished arrow needs to weigh at least 300 grains.

It's never a good idea to "dry fire" a bow, that is, to draw and release the bowstring without having an arrow on the string. Dry firing a bow can cause it to break and may injure the person who dry fires it. When you shoot an arrow that's too light for the draw weight of the bow, you

Shaft Size Selection Chart

RECURVE BOW
Finger Release

Spine charts for aluminum and carbon arrows will help you start out with the correct shaft for bare shaft tuning.

are essentially dry firing it. The excess energy not absorbed by the arrow ends up being absorbed by the limbs and riser and is felt as hand shock or recoil. Conversely, a heavier arrow absorbs much more of the bow's stored energy and allows the bow to perform to the best of its ability. A lighter arrow will fly faster and farther than a heavy arrow, so experiment with different arrow weights to see which combination performs the best with your bow. Just make sure to stay within the recommended limitations—most manufacturers won't honor their warranty if a bow has been damaged by shooting arrows that are too light.

Because of these weight considerations, you will need to decide on the weight of the field point or broadhead you will be shooting. If you're a bowhunter, choose a field point weight that matches as closely as possible the weight of the broadhead you will be using. If you don't have any idea where to start, 125 grains is a good middle-of-the-road weight. You can always come back later and experiment with arrow size and point weight after you learn the basics of bare shaft tuning. On carbon and aluminum shafts, a threaded insert is glued into the end of the shaft, and the field point or broadhead simply screws into the insert, allowing easy replacement. On wood shafts, the field point or broadhead is attached directly to the tapered end of the shaft using hot melt glue.

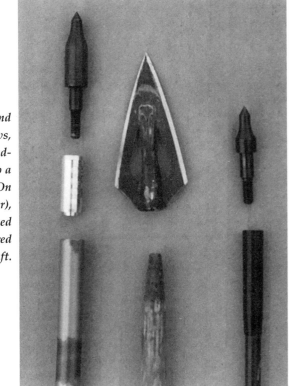

On aluminum (left) and carbon (right) arrows, the field point or broadhead screws into a threaded insert. On wood shafts (center), it should be glued directly to the tapered end of the shaft.

Once you've determined your arrow length and field point/broadhead weight, look on the spine chart to see which arrow the chart recommends. If you're looking at a chart for aluminum arrows, there will probably be three to four sizes that will shoot from your bow. There is usually a special section for traditional bows. The spine chart should also show the weight in grains of the raw arrow shaft at each length. Use this information to help you decide which shaft to choose in regard to total arrow weight, and keep in mind the manufacturer's recommendation for arrow weight per pound of draw weight. The spine charts published for carbon arrows may look different from spine charts for aluminum arrows, but they still contain the same information.

When choosing a wood shaft, remember that each end of the shaft will have to be tapered to accept a nock and field point or broadhead. Raw, unfinished wood shafts are usually 31 inches long. They are spine tested on a machine, with only 28 inches of the shaft being tested, just as the draw weight on traditional bows is measured at 28 inches. Arrow spine is dependent upon shaft length and shaft diameter. Raw shafts are sold in spine groups of 5-pound increments, such as 45–50 pounds or 50–55 pounds, and are available in the following diameters: $^1/_4$-inch, $^5/_{16}$-inch, $^{11}/_{32}$-inch, and $^{23}/_{64}$-inch. The smaller-diameter shafts are shot from bows with a lighter draw weight, and the larger-diameter shafts are shot from bows with a heavier draw weight. The spine groups themselves are based on arrow length. For instance, a 40–45 pound arrow would work for a 40-pound draw weight bow with draw lengths from 28 inches on up. The same arrow would work for a 45-pound bow with a draw length from 28 inches on down. The shorter the shaft is, the stiffer it is and the more spine it has. The longer the shaft, the more flexible it is and the less spine it has.

Let's look at this example: An archer's draw length is 29 inches and his draw weight is 55 pounds. Since wood shafts come in 5-pound spine groups, the archer could use either a 50–55 pound spine weight or a 55–60 pound spine weight. Since the archer's draw length is an inch longer than the 28-inch length the raw shaft was spined at, the archer would need a longer shaft that was still able to provide the needed spine. The 55–60 pound shaft would be the correct choice since it provides the proper spine at the archer's draw length. Another example: The archer's draw length is only 27 inches and the draw weight is still 55 pounds. The archer would need to start with a shaft that provides the proper spine at his shorter length, such as the 50–55 pound spine weight.

The easiest method for buying wood shafts is to "bracket" your target spine weight. If you need a shaft that will spine out at 55 pounds for a 28-inch arrow, then purchase two or three test shafts in each of the three spine weights close to your target weight. For example, purchase shafts spined at 45–50, 50–55, and 55–60 pounds. With all the variables that come into play, such as different limb designs and string materials, this method will help ensure that you have the correct wood shaft on hand to start out with.

Wood shafting is a lot of work, and it requires special tools to taper shafts. If you decide to use wood shafts, keep in mind the extra work involved if you make them yourself or the extra money you'll pay to buy wood arrows made by someone else.

Arrow-building equipment (such as fletching jigs and grain scales) and all arrow components are available commercially. As your skill and experience increase, you will probably decide to make your own arrows, a hobby I highly recommend. Not only does it save you money in the long run, but you also can build arrows to your own specifications much more easily than someone else can.

Nocks and Fletching

Plastic arrow nocks come in a few different styles with a size to fit each type of shaft material and shaft diameter. The throat of the nock, or the part that snaps on the bowstring, should only fit tightly enough on the bowstring to hold the arrow securely in place as the bow is drawn and the arrow released. If the nock is too tight, it makes it difficult for the arrow to come off the bowstring and affects arrow flight. If the nock is too loose on the bowstring, then the arrow may come off prematurely and cause you to dry fire the bow. Check the nock each time prior to shooting the arrow to make sure it's not cracked. A cracked nock can break during the shot and cause dry firing of the bow. You may also

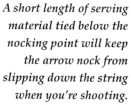

A short length of serving material tied below the nocking point will keep the arrow nock from slipping down the string when you're shooting.

find that even though the nock snaps securely onto the bowstring, it will still slide up and down the string. This can occasionally lead to arrow flight problems. To prevent this, you can either place another brass nocking point on the string directly below the arrow nock or tie a short length of serving material in that location. This will keep the arrow nock stationary during the launch of the arrow. I usually do this to all of my bowstrings, just to be safe.

Except for bare shaft tuning (see chapter 3), when you are shooting off the shelf your arrows must be fletched with feathers. Feathers will relax as they glide across the shelf rest and strike plate, then spring back to full size and shape while the arrow is in flight. Plastic vanes, though more durable and waterproof, cause the back end of the arrow to deflect off the riser and shelf because they don't give like feathers. This results in poor arrow flight.

Feathers come in four basic styles, with the first two being the most common: parabolic; traditional, or shield cut; banana; and high-profile.

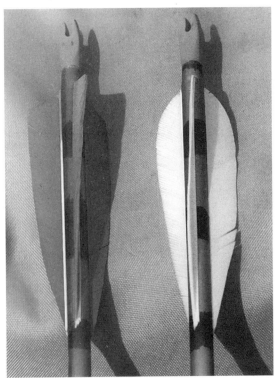

Shield cut (left) and parabolic (right) feathers. Both types work well as fletching.

When choosing what type of fletching to put on your arrows, keep in mind that for the majority of those who shoot traditional bows, 5-inch feather fletching is standard. If your shafts are tuned to your bow, then you shouldn't need any more than that. The style is more a matter of personal preference. With the exception of the high-profile design, which catches more air, stabilizes a big broadhead quickly, and slows the arrow down a bit more, all the feather styles shoot about the same.

Feathers are also available in a myriad of colors, from black to neon pink. Once again, it's a personal choice. If you are a bowhunter, I recommend shooting the brightest fletching you can find, since game animals like deer and elk don't see color like we do. This will help you follow the arrow all the way to impact and see exactly where it struck the animal. One exception: The wild turkey does see color and its eyesight is second to none, so if bowhunting turkeys, black or brown feathers work best.

Feathers, since they do come from real birds (usually farm-raised turkeys), come from either the left or right wing of the bird. The result? Left-wing or right-wing feathers. A left-wing feather will cause an arrow to spin to the left, and a right-wing arrow does the opposite. Some archers say that a right-handed shooter should have his arrows fletched with left-wing feathers, because this will cause the arrow to spin to the left and help the fletching clear the riser better. I have shot both left- and right-wing feathers from my bows, and I can tell no difference.

Feathers are applied to the arrow using a fletching jig. Insert the feather in a clamp, apply glue to the feather, and place the clamp in the jig, forcing the glued portion of the feather to contact the arrow shaft. Clamps can apply the feathers in a straight, helical, or offset fletch. Because feathers have a natural curve, the most common method of application is the helical clamp. This adds a bit more spiral to the feather than occurs naturally and imparts more spin and stabilization to the arrow in flight. Since there are left- and right-wing feathers, there are also left- and right-wing clamps. Probably 99 percent of all traditional shooters use a 5-inch feather applied with the corresponding helical clamp. You simply can't find a better combination to stabilize your arrows.

If you're just starting out, my advice is to take your arrows to an archery shop and get the feathers put on them. If you want to save some money and fletch your own arrows, however, fletching jigs and

The fletching jig is used to apply feathers to the arrow shaft.

arrow components are widely available that will allow you to do it yourself. Just be sure to read the directions carefully. With practice, it's simple to produce your own arrows that are as good as those purchased commercially.

If you plan on shooting or hunting in wet weather, you need to waterproof your feathers. While feathers do have some natural waterproofing, most of this is destroyed when they are dyed. Use a good commercially made waterproofing compound to keep your feathers from becoming saturated in wet weather. A wet feather will lie down against the shaft, providing little, if any, guidance to the arrow in flight. Of course, if you bare shaft tuned your arrows to your bow, wet feathers will create less of a problem.

Using Broadheads

For bowhunters, the hunting broadhead is just as important as the bow or arrow. It is the first thing that makes contact with the game animal

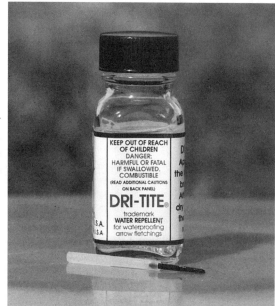

Waterproofing your feathers with a compound such as this will help them stand up better to damp weather.

and the only part of the arrow that inflicts damage. For that reason, bowhunters must be sure that their broadheads are razor-sharp and perform as intended.

The field point used for bare shaft tuning (see chapter 3) needs to be the same weight as the broadhead you intend to use. That's because a broadhead with a different weight than the field point will change the spine of the arrow and affect arrow flight. Any arrow flight problems will be magnified when shooting a broadhead, since the broadhead is much wider than a field point and catches more wind.

My personal recommendation is to use cut-on-contact two-blade broadheads, such as the ones made by Zwickey and Bear. These broadheads can be glued directly onto wood shafts, or an adapter can be glued into the broadhead, allowing it to be screwed into the insert in an aluminum or carbon arrow. These broadheads are tougher than the replaceable-blade types and cut their way through hide and muscle as opposed to punching their way through. These broadheads can be resharpened, making them more economical. Three-blade cut-on-contact broadheads are also used by many traditional bowhunters with great success. My personal preference for two-blade broadheads is

Cut-on-contact broadheads work the best with traditional equipment.

Hot melt glue will hold your broadhead firmly in place on wooden arrows.

based on many years of experience and is what works best for me and my hunting setup. Whatever brand and style you choose, make sure your broadheads fly correctly from your hunting setup before going to the woods with them. This should include checking accuracy and arrow flight characteristics all the way out to your maximum effective range.

Sharpening fixed-blade broadheads is just like sharpening a knife. Ten different hunters have ten different ways of sharpening their broadheads and their knives—anything from Arkansas stones to crock sticks to ordinary mill files. But the end result should be the same: a shaving-sharp broadhead. Don't go to the woods with anything less, and carry a sharpening device with you to touch up those broadheads in the field.

Razor-sharp broadheads and bowstrings don't mix, and during the excitement of the hunt, you may accidentally slice the bowstring with a broadhead. It happens, even to seasoned bowhunters. For that reason, always carry a spare bowstring with you when hunting. Your spare bowstring should already be broken in and be complete with a nocking point and string silencers. Also carry a bowstringer to properly string

Whatever method you use for sharpening your broadheads, make sure they are razor-sharp before heading to the field. Pictured: 1) sharpening stone, 2) hand-held sharpening device, 3) diamond hone, 4) file.

and unstring your bow while hunting. If you do happen to sever the bowstring completely, make sure there is no damage to the bow itself before replacing the string. Carrying a bowstringer and a spare bowstring can mean the difference between staying in the woods and going home early.

Arrow Speed, Weight, and Energy

Many bowhunters like to debate arrow speed versus arrow weight, with each side arguing that one is more important than the other. My thinking on the matter is this: I'd rather get hit by a feather traveling at 220 feet per second than I would by a log traveling at 175.

Another favorite topic of conversation for archers is something called FOC, or front-of-center. This refers to the amount of weight that lies forward of the center point of the arrow shaft in relation to the total weight of the arrow. Some archers, mostly tournament shooters, are concerned about FOC, while others are not. I'll describe how to figure FOC and let you decide whether it matters to you.

The theory behind FOC states that only 10 to 15 percent of the total weight of the arrow should be in front of the center point of the arrow. To figure FOC for an aluminum or carbon shaft, do this: Using a fletched shaft complete with field point or broadhead, find the spot on the shaft where it balances horizontally. Mark this spot. Then find the actual center of the shaft by measuring from the bottom of the nock groove to the end of the shaft (do not include the insert, field point, or broadhead), and divide that number by 2. Make a mark at the actual center of the shaft. Measure the distance between the two marks. Divide the distance between the two marks by the distance to the center of the shaft from one of the ends. This will be the FOC percentage. On wood arrows, the only difference in the process is the measurement of the shaft length: simply measure from the bottom of the nock groove to the edge of the glue-on field point or broadhead, and divide this by 2 to get the actual center point. All other steps are the same.

Here's an example. Say the arrow length measured from the bottom of the nock groove to the end of the shaft itself is 28 inches, the actual center point is 14 inches, and the balance point is 2 inches forward of the center point. 2 divided by 14 equals 0.143, or 14 percent. This shows that 14 percent of the total weight of the arrow lies forward of the center point of the shaft and is acceptable by FOC standards.

To determine FOC, find the balance point on the arrow and mark it.

But what does this mean? Basically, an arrow with an FOC of greater than 15 percent will nose down more quickly, while an arrow with an FOC in the 10 to 15 percent range will have a flatter trajectory. If you're like me and shoot aluminum arrows with field points and broadheads from 145 grains to 175 grains, getting an FOC between 10 and 15 percent is just not going to happen. As a matter of fact, the FOC for my arrows is up around 20 to 25 percent. Am I worried about it? No. But that's me. I refuse to spend a lot of time and money trying to get my arrows to fall within the acceptable FOC range, when the shafts I shoot right now are all bare shaft tuned and have excellent flight. Besides, none of the game animals I've taken with my bows ever knew the difference.

You may also be interested in knowing how much energy your arrows are delivering to the target. This energy, known as kinetic energy, is measured in foot-pounds. To figure the foot-pounds of energy your arrow is carrying at maximum velocity, you must know the total weight of the arrow in grains and the speed of the arrow in feet-per-second (fps). Arrow speed must be determined using a good chronograph. Shoot several arrows through the chronograph and figure the average arrow speed. Here is the formula for figuring kinetic energy of an arrow:

$$\frac{\text{arrow speed (fps) squared} \times \text{total weight of arrow (grains)}}{450{,}240} = \begin{array}{c} \text{kinetic energy} \\ \text{(foot-pounds)} \end{array}$$

Say, for example, the arrow speed is 180 fps and the total weight of the arrow is 500 grains. Squaring 180 gives you 32,400; 32,400 times 500 equals 16,200,000; and 16,200,000 divided by 450,240 equals approximately 36 foot-pounds of kinetic energy.

The end figure tells you how many foot-pounds of energy your arrow is carrying when it is traveling at the speed recorded by the chronograph. The farther the arrow travels, the more it slows down, so kinetic energy will drop accordingly.

ACCESSORIES

You should become familiar with at least a few of the accessories traditional archers use, especially the shooting glove and armguard. There are variations available for each of these, as well as a host of other neat little items that may help make your shooting more enjoyable. The following is an account of regularly used accessories, designed to make you aware of what's available. Appendix A has a partial list of suppliers of traditional archery gear, along with addresses and phone numbers.

Armguards

The armguard has been around in various forms for many years. Its two main purposes are to protect the forearm and wrist area from the bowstring and to keep bulky sleeves from catching the bowstring in cold weather. Many shooters don't wear an armguard, considering it an unnecessary inconvenience, at least until they suffer a big purple bruise on the forearm from the bowstring.

Armguards today are made from modern materials such as Velcro, nylon, and elastic, but more traditional styles made from leather are still available from traditional archery suppliers. These leather versions are available with polished bone buttons that really look sharp and do a

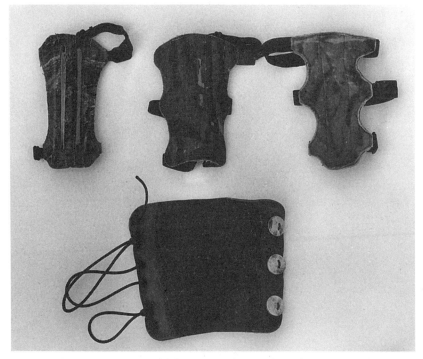

Armguards serve to protect the forearm and wrist from the occasional string slap and also keep bulky sleeves out of the way of the bowstring.

good job of protecting the arm. Many modern-day traditional shooters, myself included, enjoy making their own leather armguards. It's simple and inexpensive, and you can get just as fancy or as simple as you want.

Shooting Gloves or Tabs

A shooting glove or tab is necessary to protect the shooter's fingers from discomfort and provide a smooth, slick surface that allows the bowstring to easily slip from the fingers. A shooting glove covers the three fingers used to draw the bow, while the shooting tab has an opening that slips over the middle finger of the drawing hand. The tab has a cut-out section through which the arrow fits, and it is positioned so that the smooth surface lies between the bowstring and the fingers. I recommend you try both gloves and tabs and decide which one best suits your style of shooting and gives you the cleanest release. Each has its

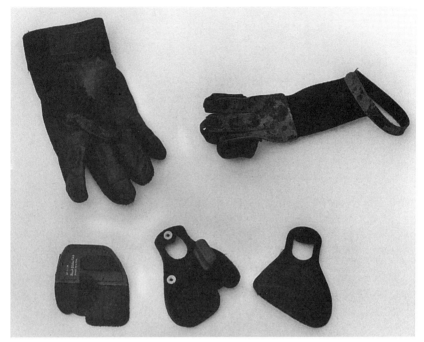

Gloves (top) and shooting tabs (bottom) protect the fingers and provide a smooth, slick surface for a clean release. Try both styles and stick with the one that works best for you.

own merits, and each is available in several variations. Both are available with either leather or hair facing in sizes to fit every hand. If you have sensitive fingers, you might want to consider a tab or glove with an extra layer of leather that protects the fingertips. If you like to feel the string, gloves are available made from deerskin, which is very thin and pliable.

Tabs and gloves are relatively inexpensive, and it pays to have two or three extras on hand, especially if you're a hunter. I lose one or two a season and have been saved on several occasions by a spare tab carried in my fanny pack.

Bow Tip Protector
The lower limb tip of your bow takes quite a bit of abuse and needs to be protected more than the upper limb tip. Any time you lean your bow

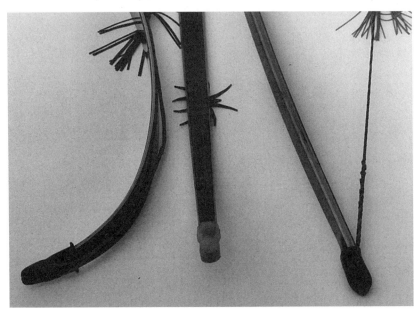

Using a bow tip protector will prevent damage to the lower limb tip when the bow is leaning against a tree.

against a tree by standing it on the lower limb tip, or rest the limb tip on the ground, you run the risk of damaging the bow tip and string loop. A bow tip protector will save wear and damage to the lower limb tip, as well as keeping the lower string loop securely in the string nock while the bow is unstrung.

Quivers

Quivers come in many styles, including hip quivers that are worn on your belt, voluminous back quivers that can carry two dozen arrows, and bow quivers that keep those arrows right there where you need them.

For me, the type of shooting I'm doing determines what kind of quiver I use. If I'm hunting, especially from a treestand, I like a good, solid bow quiver. Bow quivers are lightweight affairs that can hold anywhere from four to seven arrow shafts mounted right on the bow. A bow quiver is useful if you are wearing a daypack or carrying a portable stand that would prevent the use of a hip or back quiver. Plus, as you're

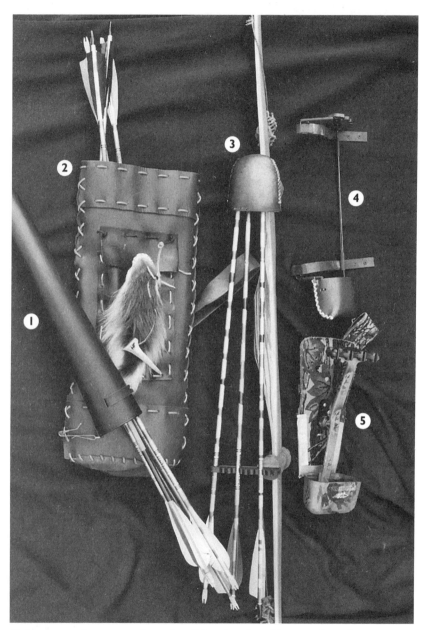

Quivers come in many styles and each has its place. They are the safest way to carry several arrows at one time. Pictured here: 1) tube-type quiver, 2) back quiver, 3) two-piece bow quiver, 4) strap-on bow quiver, 5) homemade hip quiver.

moving through thick cover, it's easier to guide your arrows through vines and the like and protect your feather fletching from damage.

If I'm out target shooting or in a 3-D tournament, I like a back quiver that can carry a lot of arrows. Getting arrows in and out of a back quiver is a lot easier than getting them in and out of a bow quiver. One of the drawbacks of using a back quiver while hunting is that the broadheads rub together and get dull rather quickly. The arrows also rattle around, causing game-spooking noise, and have a tendency to get caught on every branch or vine that you walk close to. The famous longbow shooter Howard Hill used a back quiver exclusively for his trick shooting and hunting. Hill solved the problems of noise and broadheads becoming dull by filling his back quiver about one-third full of dry oats. I've often wondered what came out of Hill's back quiver when he hunted in the rain! Another problem with using the back quiver for hunting is the motion required to reach back over the shoulder and draw an arrow.

Hip quivers are a good alternative for those who don't want to wear a back quiver and who don't want the extra weight of arrows and a quiver on the bow. There are two different types of hip quivers: one made to carry broadheads or field points, and one made to carry only field points. The one for field points only is the type normally seen at archery tournaments, with the wide belt and numerous pockets to hold score cards, pencils, and so on. These quivers usually come with separate tubes for individual arrows and have the capacity to carry as many arrows as you can make fit. The hunting hip quiver is a simple rig that holds anywhere from five to eight broadhead arrows securely on the side of the leg until they're needed. Retrieving an arrow is just a matter of reaching down and feeling for it. One of the problems with hip quivers is that the arrows occasionally get tangled up in branches and vines when you're moving through heavy cover. If you choose to use a hip quiver for hunting and you hunt from a treestand, get a hip quiver with snaps on the belt loop. Then you can undo the snaps, slide the quiver out of your belt without having to unbuckle your belt, and hang it on the side of the tree. Another alternative is to make your own hip quiver using a quiver for a compound bow. I've made one for myself using scrap leather I picked up at a local leather shop for next to nothing. Simply fashion the piece of leather into a loop that will slide over your belt, and attach to it the part of the mounting bracket for the quiver that is attached to the compound bow. Kwikee Kwivers work best for this application, because the quiver mounts on the bracket in simple fashion. Then, when you're ready to attach or remove the quiver from your belt, all you need to do is remove the quiver itself instead of the belt loop portion.

The pocket quiver isn't really a quiver in the true sense of the word. It's more like a pocket protector for archers. It consists of a leather pouch that slips down into the hip pocket of your pants and allows you to carry arrows in your hip pocket without fear of damaging your pants pocket or your backside. This quiver should be used only for the most informal shooting done in the backyard, as the arrows have a tendency to fall out if you walk very far, and it should never be used to carry broadheads.

Bow Cases

If you travel with your bow very often, especially by airplane, you'll want to invest in a good bow case. There are cases for takedown bows, one-piece bows, bows with a quiver mounted on the riser . . . just about any configuration you can imagine. For one-piece longbows, a hard tube case that does an excellent job of protecting the longbow is available from the Black Widow Bow Company (see appendix B). If you're going to spend your money on a good bow, you should spend a little extra for a case to protect it.

Chest Protector

Chest protectors are seldom seen anymore, except maybe at the Olympics and high-level archery competitions. They were widely used in days gone by as a means of keeping the shooter's shirt from getting caught in the bowstring, as well as keeping parts of the female shooter's anatomy out of the way. Consisting of a piece of leather or other material equipped with a type of harness, the chest protector simply goes over the neck and shoulder. Once adjusted properly, the chest protector covers and holds down anything that might get in the way of a bowstring. If you're experiencing bowstring interference in that area, you might want to try a chest protector.

Blunts

Blunts are special points that allow the archer to shoot at just about any object without worrying about the arrow sticking in the target. There

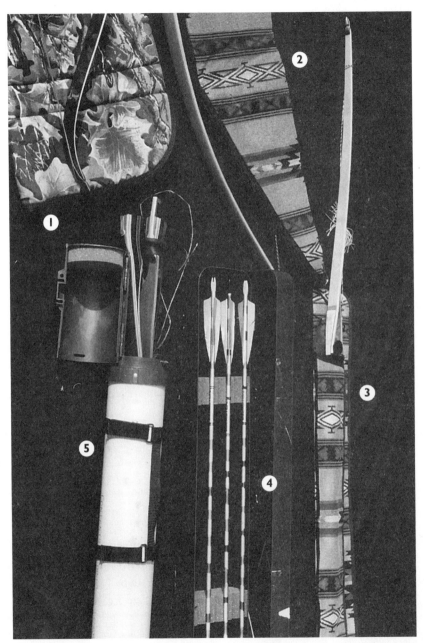

A good bow case will protect your bow while traveling. Pictured here: 1) recurve soft case with padding, 2) longbow soft case with padding, 3) longbow sleeve case, 4) styrene rubber arrow hard case, 5) tubular longbow hard case.

are several different styles to choose from, ranging from a plain rubber tip that slips over the end of the arrow to the Judo Point manufactured by Zwickey and the Shocker manufactured by Saunders. Both the Judo Point and the Shocker have spring arms that catch on grass and turf, preventing the arrow from skipping across the ground for a long distance and being lost. I've used the same point for several seasons, always managing to find my arrow no matter what I've shot it into.

Blunts can be used for target practice while you rove through the fields and woods, engaged in one of my favorite activities—stump shooting. Stump shooting is a good way to practice your instinctive shooting in a hunting environment, but shooting need not be limited to stumps. Sticks, leaves, and old corncobs are all fair game when it comes to shooting blunts.

Another advantage of blunts is that they are quite deadly on small game, up to about the size of a groundhog. One of my favorite things to do is to squirrel hunt during the latter part of deer season using Judo Points. At that time of year, squirrels are on the ground more, busying themselves with the matter of preparing for winter. Quite often, an archer can get very close to one, allowing a quick and deadly shot. When the deer hunting is slow, carry a blunt or two in your quiver for

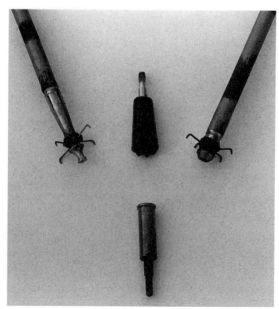

Spring-arm points (upper left and upper right) and rubber tips (top center) work well as blunts, though you can also make your own with a .38 caliber shell casing (bottom center).

small-game action and stump shooting. While the spring-arm-type points are great for small game, an alternative that works very well is to glue the casing from a .38 handgun cartridge over the end of a field point using epoxy. These homemade blunts don't have the spring-arm feature, so they're easier to lose, but they are highly effective on small game from groundhogs on down.

The Bowfit Archery Exerciser

This isn't really an accessory, but rather an exercise device designed by a physical therapist who shoots a bow. The Bowfit exerciser simulates drawing a traditional bow and is ideal for those wishing to increase their strength to shoot a bow with a heavier draw weight. It's also a great tool to use for a warmup before shooting your bow. The device uses heavy-duty bands of rubber to create resistance and has a handle similar to that of a bow. Bowfit comes in three weights: light, 10 to 40 pounds; medium, 30 to 50 pounds; and heavy, 50 to 100 plus pounds. The Bowfit costs about $22, including postage, and is available from Bowfit LLC, P.O. Box 507, Preston, ID 83263-0507, telephone (888) 757-5541, website www.bowfit.com.

There are hundreds of other neat and fascinating little items out there that, though you may not need them, make shooting more enjoyable. Most of us like to leaf through catalogs to see the latest in technology, and I'm no different. If you see something that interests you, then try it. Traditional archery is all about finding what works best for you.

- 3 -

Bare Shaft Tuning Your Bow

The goal of bare shaft tuning is to get the arrow to fly as straight as possible to the target and stick straight in, all without any fletching. Once this is accomplished and the arrow is fletched with feathers, you will have achieved near-perfect arrow flight. To bare shaft tune your bow and arrows, you will need the following:

1. Your bow.
2. One or two unfletched arrows, cut about 4 inches longer than your draw length, complete with a nock glued on and a field point of the proper weight attached.
3. Your bag target. It's important to use a bag target, because the arrows will not be flying perfectly straight during the bare shaft tuning phase, and a bag target will help prevent the shaft from being bent during impact.
4. A safe area to shoot.

Some experts claim that if you use a bow quiver, you should tune your bow and arrows with the quiver on the bow and full of arrows. If you do so without the quiver on the bow, adding the quiver could change the dynamics of the bow and cause the arrow to fly differently. It makes good sense, although I've shot a bare shaft both with the quiver on and off my bow, and I haven't seen any difference in the flight of the shaft. All bows are different, so experiment with your equipment to find out if the bow quiver makes any difference.

To get the arrow to fly fairly straight to the target without fletching requires the arrow to be the proper length and the nock location on the bowstring to be correct. All arrows, whether shot from a recurve, longbow, or flatbow, flex as they pass the bow's riser. This is known as the archer's paradox. Since the arrow shelf on most traditional bows is not cut far enough past the center of the bow to allow the arrow to fly perfectly straight from the bow, the arrow must have enough flex to allow it to bend around the riser as it passes. The amount of flex is dictated by the spine, and therefore the length, of the arrow. The shorter the arrow, the stiffer it is. The longer the arrow, the more flexible it is. For right-handed shooters, if the unfletched arrow is too stiff, it will leave the bow with the nock to the right of the field point and it will stick into the target in the same manner. If the unfletched arrow is not stiff enough, the nock will be to the left of the field point. The results will be the opposite for left-handed shooters.

This is why you start out with a full-length shaft that has been correctly selected from an arrow chart. The chart shows that the arrow you have selected, at your finished length, will be correctly spined for the bow's draw weight using the correct field point weight. Common sense says that if you start out with the shaft at full length, it will not have enough spine. By cutting off a little section of the arrow at a time, however, you will find the length at which the shaft flies from the bow and sticks in the bag target fairly straight. Once this is accomplished and fletching is added, your arrows are tuned to your bow.

The first thing you need to do is place a nocking point on your bowstring. The most common form of nocking point is a small brass band with plastic lining that clamps around the bowstring with pliers.

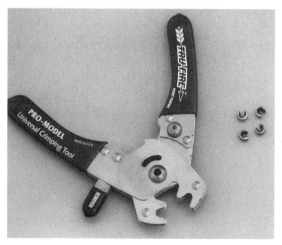

Special nock pliers squeeze the brass nock point onto the bowstring in an even manner.

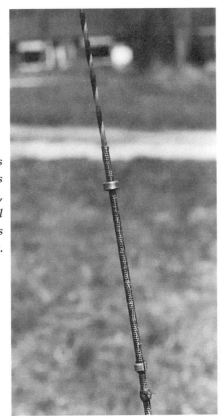

The nocking point is usually a small brass band lined with plastic, but serving material or even dental floss also works.

Special nocking point pliers do the best job of crimping the brass nocking point to the bowstring in a round, uniform manner. However, serving thread or dental floss will work just as well, provided it is securely tied to the bowstring. Start out with the nocking point about ³/₄ inch above the arrow shelf. You can eyeball this measurement or you can use a bow square. By starting out with the nocking point too high, the arrow will leave the bow with the nock above the field point and impact the target the same way. If the nocking point is too low, the arrow will fly with the nock of the arrow below the field point, or it may cause the nock end of the arrow to bounce off the arrow shelf and travel downrange with the nock high. This is very deceptive, causing you to think your nocking point is too high when, in reality, it is too

A bow square is handy for measuring how far your nocking points sits above the arrow shelf.

low. That's the reason for starting out with the nocking point in a location you know is too high: to avoid being fooled. First you work on getting the shaft the correct length to get it to fly and stick in the target fairly straight in the horizontal plane, then you gradually lower the nocking point to get rid of the nock high problem.

As your experience and understanding of the bare shaft tuning process progresses, you'll begin to understand all the variables that affect arrow flight. For instance, for a shaft that is slightly underspined (not stiff enough), a lighter field point or broadhead can be used. Less weight on the front of the arrow requires it to have less spine. For arrows that are slightly overspined, a heavier field point or broadhead can be used. More weight up front will cause the arrow to flex more as it leaves the bow.

BARE SHAFT TUNING FOR ALUMINUM
AND CARBON ARROWS

Once you have your nocking point located properly on the string, about
³/₄ inch above the shelf, then grab one of your full-length shafts that has
a nock glued on and a field point on the end. Remember, your finished
arrow length is your draw length plus 1 ¹/₂ inches. The arrow can be
longer than that, but not shorter. Measure this distance starting at the
bottom of the nock groove toward the tip of the arrow, and make a
mark on the shaft at the minimum length your arrow can be. This will
help you avoid cutting the shaft too short while tuning. Be sure to use

*Watch the mark you
made on your bare shaft.
Don't cut it too short!*

good shooting form when bare shaft tuning, as poor form may cause
arrow flight problems that confuse the tuning process. Refer to chapter
4 for specifics. Most instinctive shooters cant, or tilt, the bow to one side
to get the top limb out of the way and get a clear sight picture. During
bare shaft tuning, however, it's best to hold the bow in as close to a vertical position as possible so that you can better interpret what the arrow
is doing, both in flight and after impact. As you go through the bare
shaft tuning process, you'll see the significance of this. With the bow

Canting, or tilting, the bow to the side gets the upper limb out of the line of sight for normal shooting.

When bare shaft tuning, do not cant the bow, but hold it as close to vertical as possible.

canted, it's more difficult to tell the difference between nock high and nock left or nock low and nock right.

From a distance of 20 feet, shoot an arrow into the center of the bag target. What you're hoping for is that the arrow shaft flies to the target and sticks in with the nock to the left of the field point. If this is the case, you're on the right track. If the shaft flies and sticks in the target with the nock to the right of the field point, that means that the full-length shaft you are shooting has too much spine. You will have to either select a different shaft with less spine or shoot a much heavier field point. The best

This shaft doesn't have enough spine because it's too long, which is desirable when starting the bare shaft tuning process.

This shaft has too much spine, and it won't shoot properly from your bow.

course of action is to select a shaft with less spine. Shoot a total of five arrows to make sure that the nock left or nock right is constant. The nock of the arrow will still be too high because your nocking point is too high. You are only concerned about nock left or nock right at this time.

If your shaft is flying and impacting nock left, it's just a matter of finding the correct shaft length that imparts the correct amount of spine. Remove the insert and field point from the shaft, and cut $1/4$ inch off the end. If you're using carbon arrows, it's best to use a high-speed shaft cutter, but a clamp-type pipe-cutting tool will work if you're careful. Using a dab of hot melt glue, replace the insert and field point. Shoot the arrow five more times for consistency, noting the relationship of the nock end of the arrow to the tip of the arrow, both in flight and after impact. If the arrow is still flying and impacting nock left, then cut off another $1/4$ inch and repeat the process. Continue this process until the shaft is impacting fairly straight in the target. If you begin to see a nock

When the shaft reaches the proper length, it will stick more or less straight in the target along the horizontal plane.

right situation, you've cut too much off the shaft. Also be careful not to cut the shaft too short for your draw. Keep an eye on the mark you made on the shaft earlier. If you reach the limit line you marked on the shaft and your arrow is still impacting nock left, you'll have to start all over again with another full-length shaft with more spine than the previous shaft. Once you're satisfied with the arrow flight, move back to 20 yards and shoot the shaft again, just to confirm good arrow flight.

Once you're getting good arrow flight in the horizontal plane, it's time to work on the nocking point location. Start by moving the nocking point down the bowstring ⅛ inch. From 20 feet, shoot the arrow into the middle of the target. The nock should fly and impact lower than it previously did. Continue this process by very gradually moving the nocking point down the bowstring until the nock of the arrow is in line with the field point after impact, or at least as close as you can get it. Some people can't get rid of all the nock high because of their release or shooting style. Be very careful not to get the nocking point too low, which can cause the back end of the arrow to bounce up off the arrow shelf and make the arrow impact nock high.

Once the shaft sticks straight in the target both horizontally and vertically, then bare shaft tuning has been accomplished.

Once you've found the correct nocking point location, move back to 20 yards and shoot several arrows. Your shafts should now be flying and impacting the target fairly straight. If so, you have successfully tuned your arrows to your bow, and you are ready to add feather fletching to your shafts.

BARE SHAFT TUNING FOR WOOD ARROWS

Though wood arrows require a lot more finishing work than do carbon or aluminum, the bare shaft tuning procedures are mostly the same. There is an important difference, however. When marking your shaft to determine the minimum length it can be cut to, do not include the tapered portion of the shaft in this measurement. The field point or broadhead will cover the entire tapered portion of the shaft. If you make a mistake and include the taper in your measurement, you may end up drawing the field point or broadhead all the way up on the arrow shelf. When shortening a wood shaft, half of the taper on the point end should be cut off, then the arrow should be retapered. Glue the field point back on and shoot again. Once you've achieved good arrow flight in the horizontal plane, move on to the nocking point. Gradually move the nocking point down until you achieve good arrow flight in the vertical plane, making sure not to move it down too far. Once you've achieved good arrow flight at 20 feet, move back to 20 yards and shoot again to confirm.

- 4 -

Correct Shooting Form

Once your arrows have been tuned and your bow is properly set up, it's time to begin working specifically on shooting form. Correct shooting form is just as important as a well-tuned bow if you want to shoot accurately and consistently. While shooting style may differ among individuals, every shooter who is consistently accurate uses proper form.

Proper form can be compared with the sights on a rifle. If the sights are zeroed in and tight, and the shooter does his or her part, then the bullet will impact in the same place on every shot. However, if the front or rear sight is loose or gets moved between shots, the bullets will impact all over the target. So it is with shooting an arrow. If proper form is used consistently on every shot, the result is an arrow that's on target. If there is a mistake on your part, the arrow will not go where you want it to. It is very important to learn and practice proper shooting form in the beginning in order to help build a proper foundation to continue as a successful instinctive shooter.

BASIC REQUIREMENTS FOR PROPER FORM

There are nine basic requirements for proper shooting form. While these nine steps may seem like a lot to remember, they take only a few seconds to accomplish in reality, especially after you practice them for a while. In the beginning, every motion should be deliberate and thought out, following the guidelines for proper shooting form. Early on, you're building muscle memory and working on good habits. Practice your proper shooting form until it becomes second nature. Then you can put all your concentration on the target, where it belongs.

Stance

Your stance, or how you address the target, is important, because in order to properly make use of your upper-body strength to draw the bow, you must be balanced below the waist. Begin by facing your body at a 45-degree angle to the target. If you are a right-handed shooter, your right shoulder will be back with your left shoulder toward the target. If you are a left-handed shooter, your left shoulder will be back and your right foot forward, toward the target. In either case, your back foot should be parallel to the face of target, and your front foot

A solid stance is the foundation of good shooting form.

should point the same direction as your body. The feet should be slightly more than shoulder width apart for stability. Bend the front knee slightly, and place about one-third of your body weight on the front foot. This position allows you to turn your upper body right or left, bend forward or back at the waist, and still maintain balance. When shooting at a target that is uphill or downhill, it is important to always bend at the waist to line up the shot. Never raise or lower the bow arm itself, because this will change your sight picture and cause the arrow to fly either high or low.

Always bend at the waist when shooting higher or lower.

Grip

If you grip your bow too tightly, you may torque or twist it, causing poor arrow flight, and you may miss the target to the right or left. If you don't grip it tightly enough, you may drop it when you release the arrow. The bow should be held in a firm manner, with the arrow shelf in line with the bones of the wrist and forearm. If you trace the arrow

A firm grip on the bow is all that's required. Not too tight, not too loose.

shelf from front to back, you should find that the line corresponds to the line of the bones in your wrist. This provides the most stability and strength and promotes even pressure over the joints involved. The shape of your bow's grip will also determine how it fits your hand. Bows may have a high, medium, or low wrist grip—see pages 7–8 for more details.

Draw

There are several different schools of thought on how to properly draw the bow. Some shooters prefer to start with the bow pointed downward and bring it up as they draw and anchor. Others claim the best method is to start with the bow pointed up at about a 40-degree angle and bring it down as you draw and anchor. My personal preference and recom-

Start the draw with the bow and arrow aimed at the target, not pointed up or down.

mendation is this: Start out with the bow and arrow pointed directly at the target, and draw the bow straight back in a smooth, deliberate manner to the anchor point. This is an especially good method if you're a bowhunter, as there is much less movement involved. Incidentally, this is a good way to see if someone is trying to shoot a bow with a draw weight that is too heavy. The archer will inevitably point the bow skyward and go through wild gyrations as he or she fights to come to full draw. If you can't draw the bow straight back smoothly and deliberately, then you're shooting too much draw weight.

The bowstring should be located in the crease of the first joint on all three fingers used to draw the bowstring, with all three creases aligned. Just as important is the fact that equal pressure should be applied to the bowstring by all three fingers in order to apply even pressure to the nock of the arrow. Placing the bowstring in the creases of the finger joints causes a slight hook effect, which requires less hand and arm strength to hold on to the bowstring and prevents torque on the bowstring that would cause poor arrow flight. This also allows the drawing hand and forearm to relax a little, and causes the back muscles to do the work as they should. Proper shooting form brings the shot into alignment; the back muscles, and not the hand and arm muscles, do the pulling and maintain the tension on the bowstring.

If you find yourself having problems getting a clean release when shooting with the bowstring in the creases of the first finger joints, check to make sure that your shooting glove or tab has not developed a groove where the bowstring makes contact. This groove can develop over time and causes the bowstring to get hung up, even though you make a good release. If you find a groove in your tab or glove, it's time to replace it. If you're still having problems getting a clean release, try moving the bowstring a little more toward the tips of the fingers. This will require a little more finger and arm strength, as well as extra attention to providing equal pressure by all three fingers on the bowstring.

Steady Bow Arm

Consider the bow arm to be the equivalent of the front sight of a rifle. If you're at full draw and your bow arm is waving around or shaking too much, the arrow flight will be affected and you won't hit what you're aiming at. Once you're at full draw and anchored, that bow arm should be as steady as a rock until the arrow hits the target. You need to put a little bend in the elbow to help turn the forearm out of the way of the bowstring. Bending the elbow also helps prevent excessive strain on the elbow joint, which can cause injury.

Anchor and Anchor Point

There are different schools of thought on the proper anchor point. It depends largely on what shooting style you use. The three-fingers-under grip, where all three fingers used to draw the bow are under the arrow, will bring the arrow shaft up closer to the eye. A good anchor point for this style of shooting is to place the tip of the index finger in

The bow arm should stay steady through the draw and after the shot.

the corner of your mouth. If you shoot split fingers—one finger above and two below the arrow—try placing the tip of the middle finger in the corner of the mouth. Not every shooter has the same head size or shape or the same finger length, so you will have to determine the best location for you to use as an anchor point. The important thing is that your anchor point be the same every time. A consistent anchor point will lead to consistent accuracy.

Once you anchor, the forearm of the drawing hand should be in line with the arrow shaft, and the elbow should be in line with the anchor point and the bow hand. Consider this to be the rear sight of the rifle. Head position is an important part of the anchoring process as well. The arrow shaft should be lined up under the eye. To accomplish this, tilt your head down and tuck your chin to bring the arrow shaft into alignment directly under the right eye, if you are a right-handed shooter.

How long you hold at anchor is up to you. If the shot is lined up and feels good, then release the arrow. If not, hold at anchor until you're ready. If you start to shake or can't get the shot lined up, let the bow down. Nothing says that once you've drawn the bow you must release.

A good anchoring technique for split-fingered shooters is to place the tip of the middle finger in the corner of the mouth.

Proper alignment of the bow hand, anchor point, and elbow is necessary for correct shooting form.

Sight Picture

The sight picture is something you will develop as you gain experience with instinctive shooting. Your eyes see the target, your brain gauges the distance and sends a message to the body, and the body responds by lining up the shot. Once your skills are sufficiently developed, this whole process takes only a split second. But these skills take time and repetition to develop. Before you ever draw the bow, your eyes should focus on the exact spot where you want the arrow to go. Focus on that spot until it is the only thing you see clearly. Concentration and focus are the keys to developing your sight picture.

Some instinctive shooters use an aiming method known as gap shooting. I'm not going to teach it because I don't use it, but you should be aware of it nonetheless. In gap shooting, the archer uses the tip of the field point or broadhead as a sight pin, holding the tip either above or below the target, depending on the distance from the target. The closer to the target the shooter is, the further below the target the point is held. The farther away from the target, the higher the tip is held. The distance at which the tip is held directly on the target with the arrow striking the target is known as point of aim. This system, while not actually using a sight mounted directly to the bow, still requires the shooter to know the distance to the target. It is used by a lot of tournament shooters when an accurate estimation of distance can be made.

Breath Control and Release

These two requirements occur almost simultaneously. Studies have shown that if you are inhaling as you release the arrow, your shot will be high. If you are exhaling when you release, the shot will be low. Does this mean you should hold your breath? Yes, but only long enough to shoot the arrow. This exercise works great not only for target shooters, but also for hunters who need to calm their nerves before making a shot on a game animal. First take a deep breath and slowly let it out. Take another, let it out halfway and hold it, then draw, anchor, and release. Another method, used by rifle shooters and also taught in the military, is to let your breath out all the way without forcing any extra out, and hold it for the split second needed to make the shot.

A clean release is required for good arrow flight. Once at anchor, do not allow the bowstring to creep forward. The fingers should be extended, not curled into a fist. To achieve the cleanest possible release and make use of the bow's stored energy, maintain constant back tension. Once you reach anchor, concentrate on the target and use the back muscles to bring the elbow of the drawing arm back while allowing the bowstring to slip evenly off the fingers. By continuing to bring the elbow back, you force the drawing hand and fingers out and away from the anchor point and allow the bowstring to slip cleanly away.

Some instinctive shooters never even hesitate at anchor, while others hesitate momentarily, then continue to bring the elbow back and release the bowstring. Regardless of how long you wait, maintain constant back tension and never let the bowstring creep forward once you've reached the anchor point.

Follow-Through

The follow-through is nothing more than allowing the drawing hand to travel backward after the release in a natural manner. The bow arm should stay steady until the arrow impacts the target, and your eyes should follow the arrow all the way to the target.

Allow the hand to travel straight back after release.

WARMUPS

In order to further develop your shooting form, I recommend the following warmups and exercises. All athletes warm up before taking part in strenuous exercise. Shooting a bow may not be strenuous exercise for most people, but it does place strain on muscles and joints. Have you ever picked up a bow and noticed how your muscles and joints groan a little the first time you draw it back? That's because you're placing a load on them that they're not quite prepared for, and you are risking serious, perhaps permanent, injury. By simply taking a moment or two before you start your shooting session to warm up, not only will you lessen your risk of injury, but you'll also notice your first few shots will be more accurate.

I recommend warming up not only the shooting muscles, but the entire body, to get the blood flowing. Start out by doing jumping jacks for 30 to 45 seconds. This exercise utilizes the entire body and is a great way to loosen up the shoulders. I realize that some folks are self-conscious about doing jumping jacks in public, and that's understandable. An alternative, though not as good as jumping jacks, is simply to draw your bow back in small increments until you can reach full draw without any discomfort. If you have a better method of warming up, then do it. Just make sure your body is prepared to handle the load of repeatedly drawing your bow.

SHOOTING FORM EXERCISE #1

This exercise does not involve nocking or shooting an arrow, but it is very important to building correct shooting form. All you need is your bow and a mirror. Simply take up a correct stance, then draw, anchor, and slowly let the bow down. Watch yourself in the mirror. Are you meeting the requirements for correct shooting form? Practice this exercise until you are comfortable in your knowledge of what good shooting form feels like. If you notice yourself lacking in one of the requirements, practice proper shooting form until you've corrected the problem. Once you're ready, go to Exercise #2.

SHOOTING FORM EXERCISE #2

For this exercise, you'll need your bow, one arrow, and your bag target. Hang the bag target at chest level and be sure that you have a safe backstop. Stand back from the target at a distance from which an arrow will

*Up-close "bag work" with your eyes closed helps you focus on your
shooting form.*

immediately impact the target when shot. Stand just far enough back that the arrow will clear the bow.

This exercise consists of shooting an arrow into the bag target with your eyes closed. This is the *only* time you should ever shoot an arrow with your eyes closed. The reason for doing this is to allow you to work on all the aspects of good shooting form without the outside distraction of vision and without having to worry about where your arrow hits.

First, take up a good stance in front of the target, making sure that the arrow will impact the target when you release it. Now, raise the bow, close your eyes, and shoot the arrow using correct shooting form. Concentrate only on shooting form. While your eyes are closed, check yourself mentally and physically as you come to full draw and anchor to make sure that you're meeting the requirements of good shooting form. Everything is internalized here. Let your mind absorb what it feels like as you go through the motions. If you feel yourself doing something wrong, stop shooting and go back to Exercise #1 until you get the problem corrected. If your problem is with the release, you obviously are going to have to shoot an arrow to correct that, so work on the release until it's smooth.

I recommend that you continue with Exercise #2 until you've shot at least 800 to 1,000 arrows in this manner. I also recommend shooting five to ten arrows as described in Exercise #2 before every practice session from here on out. You cannot be a consistent, accurate, instinctive shooter until you have the fundamentals of correct shooting form ingrained in your mind to the point that they become automatic. Do not overdo it. Don't try to shoot all 800 to 1,000 in one day or even five days. Pace yourself. Practice your shooting form only as long as you can maintain the discipline necessary to perform each action correctly. Once you've completed at least 800 to 1,000 shots using correct shooting form, and you're comfortable that your shooting form is correct, go on to the next chapter.

- 5 -

Basic Accuracy Exercises

Once you have practiced your shooting form to the point where it is second nature and no longer requires conscious thought to properly execute, you can continue working on the sight picture and accuracy. You probably won't hit the bull's-eye on the first few shots, even though they'll be from a very short distance. That's perfectly fine. Your mind and body want the arrow to go to the bull's-eye, but they haven't worked together enough yet to learn how to do it consistently. By practicing a series of progressive steps using correct shooting form, you'll build the foundation required to do that. The human body is a wonderful machine in that it teaches itself to perform a task and learns from its mistakes.

In the phased exercises that follow, you are shooting from a known distance. This is just to give you a consistent reference point to shoot from in the beginning. As your skill and experience increase, knowing the distance to the target will not be necessary, because your shot will be based on your sight picture, not yardage. Your eyes will focus on the target, and your brain will analyze the information and send a message to the body. The body will follow directions and make the necessary adjustments to send the arrow to the target. Ultimately, there is no need to know how many yards it is to the target. You will also discover later on that your accuracy falls off at a certain distance. The farthest distance you can shoot an arrow accurately and consistently is known as your maximum effective range.

For the basic accuracy exercises, you'll need your bow, one arrow, and your bag target. Place your target in an area with a safe backstop at

A two-inch circle may look small, but it will help your focus and concentration at close range.

about chest level. Using a black marker, make a circle two inches in diameter in the center of the target. The reason for such a small target is that you will be close to it when you shoot, and a smaller target makes you concentrate more. Also, if you're a bowhunter, this will help you to concentrate on picking out a specific spot to shoot at on an animal, instead of shooting at the whole animal. Concentration will become a big factor from here on out, so make sure you're not distracted by anything and that you don't get in a rush to shoot the arrow.

You will only be shooting one arrow at a time during these exercises in order to give you a clean target to concentrate on, and to prevent you from shooting off nocks or otherwise damaging arrows. Warm up before beginning each shooting session, and don't push your body and brain past their limitations. If you become tired or frustrated, back off and give it a rest. These basic exercises should be enjoyable. Try to shoot a few "eyes-closed" shots up close to refresh your shooting form before starting these exercises.

PHASE ONE

The distance from the target for this first phase is 5 feet. No more, no less. At this distance, take up a proper stance in front of the target. Focus your vision on the black circle in the center of the target. Stare at

5 ft.   Phase One

10 ft.   Phase Two

20 ft.   Phase Three

40 ft.   Phase Four

60 ft.   Phase Five

Basic Accuracy Exercises

the circle intently until everything in your peripheral vision begins to blur. Bring the bow up, still focusing your vision on the circle. Draw, anchor, and shoot an arrow at the center of the black circle using proper shooting form. Note where the arrow impacted. Pull the arrow and shoot it again. Don't worry if you're not hitting the circle; your brain and body want the arrow to impact in the circle, and right now they're learning how to do that. If your arrow is consistently striking high or low, then lower or raise the plane of the arrow by bending at the waist. If the arrow is impacting to the right or the left, then try tilting the bow more or less than you did previously, or pivot slightly left or right at the waist. The actual physical movement required to change the impact of the arrow at this distance is so small you may not even notice you did it. As long as you are using proper shooting form, your body more than likely will make the correct adjustments on its own.

Continue this exercise until you can place nine out of ten arrows inside the two-inch circle at five feet, and you have shot a minimum of 500 arrows inside the circle. Hitting the bull's-eye 500 times at that range ensures that you have shot enough arrows and have received

Concentrate and try to put the arrow in the center of the two-inch circle.

enough positive reinforcement to make that sight picture and the resulting muscle responses come into play every time you shoot from that distance. This is a very important phase in the learning process, so don't cheat yourself or push too hard. Don't worry about how long it takes to shoot those 500 arrows inside the circle; learning ability and skill retention differ from archer to archer. Just continue to use good shooting form. Hard work and a positive attitude will be rewarded. You might not be comfortable quitting at that particular range after shooting 500 bull's-eyes and may want to continue there for a while longer in order to reinforce the sight picture. Once you have successfully completed your minimum of 500 shots in the circle *and* you're comfortable with your shooting, move on to phase two.

PHASE TWO
The exercise here is the same as for phase one, except this time you'll be shooting at 10 feet, twice the distance of phase one. That doesn't seem like much of a jump, but you'll see when you shoot that first arrow that the comfort zone is now smaller than it was. Remember to warm up

properly and practice the shooting form drill with your eyes closed before each shooting session.

As in phase one, continue shooting at this distance until you can place nine out of ten arrows inside the circle and have shot a minimum of 500 bull's-eyes. Shoot only one arrow at a time, and take your time between shots. Execution of proper shooting form and building that sight picture are the focus of these exercises. Once you have placed your 500 shots inside the circle and are satisfied with your shooting ability, move on to the next phase.

PHASE THREE

In this phase, you double the shooting distance again, all the way out to 20 feet. The same rules apply here. Warm up and practice correct shooting form before beginning your shooting session. You'll notice that the two-inch circle is starting to look smaller now. Good. The smaller the target, the greater the amount of concentration required to hit it. You'll also notice your sight picture looks different again. You're probably seeing more space between you and the target in your peripheral vision. Block that out by concentrating on the circle until everything else is blurry. Nothing has changed except the distance, and you can shoot three arrows here to avoid walking back and forth between the target so much. Again, continue with this exercise until you are able to keep nine out of ten arrows inside the circle at 20 feet. Don't worry about how long it takes you to accomplish this. This is a learning process and you will succeed. Once you're confident at this distance and you've shot 500 arrows inside the circle, move on to the next phase.

PHASE FOUR

Double the distance again to 40 feet from the target. At this distance, drop the bag target down from chest level to waist level. Take your black marker and enlarge the circle to four inches. Remember, 40 feet is only 13 yards—no big deal. Just keep using good shooting form and don't forget to warm up and practice correct shooting form prior to beginning each shooting session. The requirements are the same for a passing grade in this phase: once you can keep nine out of ten arrows inside the circle and have successfully shot 500 bull's-eyes, you are ready for the next phase.

At 40 feet, make the circle four inches in diameter to aid focus and concentration.

PHASE FIVE

This phase of the basic accuracy exercise has less of an increase in distance than the previous phases, because you're reaching distances that may be the maximum effective range for some shooters. In this phase, you'll be shooting at a distance of 60 feet, which is 20 yards. The same rules apply as before. Correct shooting form and concentration are critical here and can mean the difference between an arrow landing inside the circle and just outside of it. Continue this exercise until you can keep nine out of ten arrows inside the circle and place 500 bull's-eyes. It's getting a little more challenging now, isn't it? But you're getting better, too. It doesn't matter if you reach this phase in two weeks or two months. The important thing is that the combination of correct shooting form and repetitive shooting is training your brain and body how to shoot instinctively, and how to do it correctly. Shoot every arrow as if hitting inside the circle were the most important thing in the world, and you only have one chance to do it.

ADDITIONAL PHASES

You may wish to add another phase or two to increase the distance still further. Increase the distance no more than 15 feet at a time, and observe the same requirements set forth in the other phases before increasing distance. I would not recommend shooting at a distance past 25 or 30 yards in the early stages of your learning, because you'll overload your brain with input.

Different shooters' skills and abilities develop at different rates. Do not get in a big hurry. Each phase of this program has the same purpose: to teach yourself to shoot instinctively. If you follow this plan faithfully, as it's written, you will become successful.

Any time you become bored, frustrated, or mentally or physically tired, take a break. The break can be anywhere from a few minutes to a couple of days—however long it takes to recuperate and regain a positive mental approach.

Completion of the basic accuracy exercises does not mean that you can't learn any more, or that you have gone as far as you can, or that you can quit practicing. Regular, correct practice will keep your eye sharp and your shooting muscles toned. The advanced accuracy exercises in the next chapter will present more challenges and the opportunity to put together everything you've learned up until now.

- 6 -

Advanced Accuracy Exercises

By now, you should be competent and confident in the use of your equipment and in your shooting skills. For these exercises, you'll need the same equipment as before, except you will now need five arrows instead of four. At this point, you might find that a cheap tube quiver, the kind that hangs from your belt, will come in handy to carry your arrows.

If your bag target is getting worn out from repeated shooting into the same area, you can draw the four-inch circle somewhere else on the target or use the other side. The bag target I'm shooting now is four years old and still serviceable, because I switch sides on a regular basis.

PHASE ONE
This first phase is somewhat similar to the basic accuracy exercises, except you won't be shooting from the same distance on every shot. This is where you'll put it all together and find out if you've practiced enough to get that sight picture ingrained in your mind. Again, you'll be shooting at a four-inch circle on the bag target.

As usual, start out with a thorough warmup and practice correct shooting form. Then move to a spot about 60 feet from the target. The first shot will be taken from 60 feet, the second shot from five feet, the third shot from 40 feet, the fourth shot from 10 feet, and the last shot from 20 feet. The distances are mixed up in order to stimulate your brain to recall all the sight picture information you've stored from the previous shots you've made. When you shoot from one distance for a long period of time, it becomes easier because you get into a groove and that sight picture stays in your brain. However, if you shoot from a different distance on every shot, it makes your brain work harder and draw on more information to get the correct sight picture.

You should be able to keep four out of five arrows inside the four-inch circle on each series of shots. This phase enables you to identify what distances, if any, you're having accuracy problems with. Then you can go back and address the problem distances with the appropriate phases from the basic accuracy exercises. There will be no minimum number of arrows from here on out, because your foundation should be built by now. If you have found a distance that gives you problems, go back and work on it until you are competent at that distance again. Also, if you added an extra phase or two in the basic accuracy exercises, add a couple more arrows to your quiver, and include those distances in this phase. Once you are consistently hitting the mark at each of the given distances, move on to the next phase.

PHASE TWO
Now you are going to do away with known distances and start shooting from anywhere within your maximum effective range.

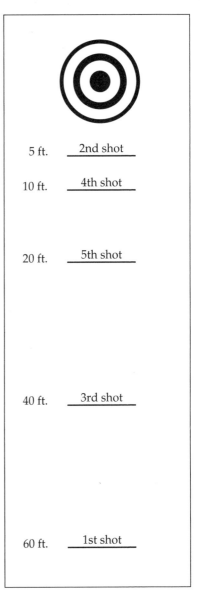

5 ft.	2nd shot
10 ft.	4th shot
20 ft.	5th shot
40 ft.	3rd shot
60 ft.	1st shot

Advanced Accuracy Exercises,
Phase One

This is the final phase. Start out standing with your back against the target. Take four steps away from the target. Turn around and shoot an arrow, taking your time and using correct shooting form. Once that arrow has been shot, turn around and take five steps away from the first spot, then turn around and shoot another arrow. Continue in this fashion until you reach your maximum effective range, mixing up the number of steps between shots. This is to help you become accustomed to shooting at a distance you haven't shot from before, and to keep you from subconsciously gravitating to the distances at which you're most comfortable. Commonly called roaming, this is perhaps the best and most basic type of instinctive shooting practice you can make use of.

These advanced accuracy exercises are really nothing more than organized, fundamental archery practice designed for instinctive shooters who are competent with their equipment. As you progress in skill and experience, include these two phases in organized practice to keep yourself from shooting only within your comfort zone. Though you likely will develop your own favorite methods of practicing your instinctive shooting skills, make sure you include the proper fundamentals. Proper practice on a regular basis throughout your archery career will help you shoot your best every time out, whether it's from the target stake or the treestand.

- 7 -

Instinctive Bowhunting Practice

The bowhunter's heart was pounding in his chest as he studied the big bull elk feeding in the tangled aspen thicket. Though the bull was a mere 15 yards away, its vital zone was covered by a cluster of vines. Down on one knee, the bowhunter realized that if he bent forward slightly at the waist, an opening appeared in the vines directly over the bull's chest cavity. The hunter knew that by bending forward and holding his longbow horizontally, he could send a shaft cleanly through the opening and into the bull's chest cavity. He knew this because he had practiced this shot many times before . . . in his backyard. Focusing his concentration on a tuft of dark-colored hair behind the bull's shoulder, the hunter took a deep breath, drew, and released the shaft in a fluid motion. The elk, hearing a dull thump, looked down to see vivid yellow feathers protruding from its rib cage. That was one of the last things it saw as the razor-sharp broadhead did its job, putting the bull down for good less than 50 yards from the hunter.

While the events described above were created to make a point, there's no doubt that similar scenarios have played out for hundreds of years. The hunter in this story might have made several mistakes, or he might simply not have realized a good shot opportunity because he didn't know what his bow was capable of, or simply because he was excited. The exercises below will test your shooting ability during periods of raised cardiovascular activity and help you create shooting scenarios that you may encounter while hunting. If you practice making difficult shots at home, and give your bow a real wringing out to see what its capabilities are, you may find yourself presented with more shot opportunities in the woods.

To get the full benefit of this type of instinctive shooting practice, you need a two- or three-dimensional animal target that is made to look like the species you intend to hunt. As far as I can tell, nearly every species of animal that is hunted has an ethafoam counterpart manufactured by one of today's 3-D target manufacturing companies. These targets, depending on manufacturer, come in a wide range of prices to suit

3-D targets provide realistic practice for hunting season.

most shooters' wallets. Flat, 2-D targets are also available for a lower price and still give the basic silhouette of the game animal. If you can't afford either of these, don't despair. Create your own silhouette game animal from some large pieces of cardboard, tape, and colored markers, and fasten it to the front of your bag target. You can invest as much or as little in a target as you like. One word of caution, though: Unless you're in a 3-D archery tournament, disregard the scoring rings on the

3-D target, as most targets don't have these accurately placed to reflect the true location of the vital organs in a game animal. Some, however, do show anatomical structure such as bones. If you're not familiar with where the internal organs in your game animal are located, go to the library and do research.

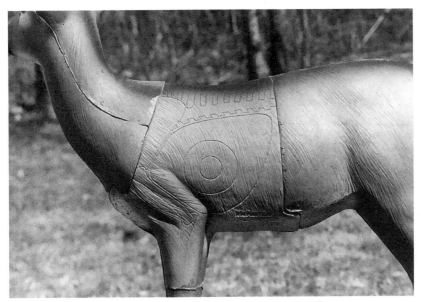

While the tournament scoring rings on most 3-D targets don't reflect the correct place to shoot a live animal, some targets will show outlines of the animal's anatomy to help bowhunters with arrow placement.

You'll need your bow and arrows set up exactly the way they would be if you were hunting. If you hunt with a bow quiver, practice with one full of arrows. Also practice with your hunting clothes on, complete with gloves and a headnet if you use them. You should make this exercise as realistic as possible, and shooting with your hunting setup and clothing will enable you to take care of any problems that might arise before hunting season.

If you're shooting at a foam target and want to shoot an occasional broadhead or two, that's fine, though you should be very careful to have a safe backstop behind the target. Don't shoot a broadhead into your bag target—it not only reduces the life of the target, it is also dangerous, as the arrow may pass completely through the bag target and travel beyond it. Also, broadhead-tipped arrows are difficult to remove from a bag target because the broadhead becomes entangled in the material. If you're shooting broadheads, I recommend shooting only one arrow at a time to save money on replacing arrows and components.

If you hunt from a treestand, practice shooting from an elevated position, if possible. Shooting from higher up has a tendency to cause the arrow to fly high, so you will find that you have to shoot at a point slightly lower than the intended point of impact. If you don't think about this and practice it, then you'll shoot high on the game animal when the chips are down. Remember to always bend at the waist when shooting uphill or downhill. Never elevate or drop that bow arm, or your sight picture will be off.

EXERCISE ONE: THE GUT CHECK

As anybody who has ever bowhunted knows, when a game animal comes within bow range, your body undergoes physical changes. Your breathing and heart rate increase, your blood pressure goes up, and your concentration falters. Though you can't shoot at live animals in a practice environment, you can attempt to reproduce the physical effects of the adrenaline rush you get when encountering game. Place your bow, with an arrow nocked, on the ground at a reasonable distance from the target. At a good pace, run 50 feet away from the bow, stop and do thirty jumping jacks, then run back to your bow. Pick up the bow and, using correct shooting form, attempt to place an arrow in the kill zone of the animal target. By the time you get back to your bow, you should notice an increase in breathing and heart rate. If not, you wimped out on the physical exercise. Try this exercise a few times to get the feel of shooting instinctively while under cardiovascular stress. Be sure to rest sufficiently between sessions, and don't try to shoot if you're too tired.

Keep in mind that it's always a good idea to consult your physician before performing this or any other strenuous exercise.

EXERCISE TWO: WRINGING OUT YOUR BOW

Traditional shooters often go many years not realizing that their bows are capable of some pretty amazing feats and can be shot in a number of different positions. The longbow, especially, is a very forgiving piece of equipment. It can be held horizontally, vertically, or even upside down and will still send a shaft to the mark accurately and with power. On ESPN's "American Shooter" and TNN's "Everything Outdoors," Byron Ferguson, using longbows he makes himself, has done everything from shooting an aspirin out of the air to banking arrows off plywood walls to breaking balloons. The recurve, too, deserves credit for an amazing amount of versatility.

The point is, you can shoot your bow from more than just the standing position. While the requirements for good shooting form still apply, you'll find ways to modify your shooting form and still get good arrow flight and accuracy. The two most common alternative shooting positions are kneeling and sitting, and you can incorporate them into your bowhunting practice. Though these are not by any means the only other positions you can shoot a bow from, they are the most stable.

Kneeling
The kneeling position is a good way to shoot under an object or just to lower your profile while hunting on the ground. If done correctly, the kneeling position will provide stability and a wide range of movement.

On uneven terrain, extending a leg to one side can add balance and stability during the shot.

When shooting from the kneeling position, you can either sit on your heels (top) or rise up on your knees for added elevation (bottom).

There are a couple of different positions that can be used. The first is simply to kneel on both knees, with the knees slightly more than shoulder width apart for stability. The second is to kneel on the left knee (for right-handed shooters) and extend the right leg out to the side. In both of these positions, you can either rest your rear on your heel(s) or rise up onto your knee(s) for a little more elevation.

Practice shooting a few arrows into your bag target from this position at close range to familiarize yourself with how it feels and the changes you need to make in your shooting style.

Sitting

One morning many years ago, after I first started hunting with traditional equipment, a nice whitetail doe walked downhill in front of me at about 15 yards. The doe put her head down and started to feed on acorns, presenting me with an ideal broadside shot. The only problem was, I was sitting against a tree with my legs crossed. At that time, I

With practice, traditional bows can be shot accurately from a sitting position.

never even considered attempting to shoot from that position because I didn't think it could be done. As I slowly moved around to get up on my knees, the doe's head came up and she caught me in an awkward position. Every muscle was straining to hold still, but she decided she didn't like my company and headed to the next county. In frustration, I sat back down against the tree. As I stared down the hill at the oak tree that the doe had been feeding under, I started to wonder if I could have made that shot while sitting. I pulled a blunt-tipped arrow from my quiver, picked out a spot on the side of the oak tree at the same level as the doe's chest, and proceeded to center-punch the spot. From that point on, I practiced shooting from the sitting position on a regular basis.

Shooting a bow from the sitting position will feel strange at first because you're using some muscles not ordinarily involved. You'll also have to cant the bow more to prevent the lower limb tip from striking the ground. You can have your legs either crossed or straight out in front of you. It doesn't make much difference as long as you can maintain balance. There's really not much to it, except to practice. You might find the need to shoot from this position sometime, so give it a try.

Other Positions
You can also shoot your bow from the prone position, on your back, twisted around the side of a tree, and just about any other way imagina-

Learning to shoot your bow from every position will open up shot opportunities in the field.

ble. Experiment for yourself, and shoot your bow from every possible position you can think of. If you don't, you'll never realize your full potential as an instinctive shooter, and you'll never learn what your bow is capable of. Just be sure to shoot safely with a good backstop.

EXERCISE THREE: THREADING THE NEEDLE

If you bowhunt long enough, you will eventually run into a situation, like the hunter in the opening story, where you need to send an arrow through a small opening. The best way to be prepared for this situation is to practice it. This can be done from a treestand or on the ground, and from any shooting position.

Place your animal target in a location where it is screened by a tree or bush. If you don't have a tree or bush, use whatever you can find. Try to place the animal so that there is only a small opening over the vital organs. Practice shooting through that opening from a variety of positions, such as sitting, kneeling from behind cover, and so on. Try

Practicing the shot beforehand will help you "thread the needle" on that big buck.

making the shot after some brief exercise to elevate your heart and breathing rates. Use your imagination. Create different scenarios to challenge your shooting skills and to help you prepare for situations you might encounter while hunting. Practice quartering-away shots on your animal target. In a quartering-away shot, the animal target is almost perpendicular to your line of sight, except its hindquarters are slightly closer to you than its head. This is really helpful on a lifelike target, because it allows the most access to the animal's vitals and lets you see what organs you would have struck on a real animal.

The keys to "threading the needle" are to have your equipment properly tuned so that the arrow stabilizes quickly after leaving the bow, and to concentrate fully on the spot where you want the arrow to hit. An improperly spined arrow will still be fishtailing when it reaches the opening and may be deflected. Focus on the spot on the animal where the arrow needs to go, not on the opening itself.

Game animals—except for the wild turkey—don't see color as we do, but their visual acuity is so great that they can pick out small movements from a long distance. To successfully draw your bow on a game animal, wait until the animal's vision is blocked or its head is down. In order to keep your movement to a minimum while drawing the bow, point the bow at the animal as it approaches, and follow it as it moves. When the time comes for the shot, the bow and arrow will already be on target. Then all that's left is to draw the bow straight back, anchor, and make a good shot. Following the animal with the arrow will keep you from having to swing the bow around to get on target. The drawing arm will be moving straight back, and the movement will be partially blocked by the bow. Practice picking a spot; drawing in a slow, smooth, deliberate manner; and making the shot. I recommend picking a spot on the game animal as soon as it comes within range, and concentrating on that spot only. Avoid the temptation of gazing at antlers or beards. Many antlers have been pierced and beards shot off by the arrows of hunters who, instead of picking a spot, were looking in the wrong place. Their arrows went where their concentration was focused.

TOURNAMENTS AND TARGET SYSTEMS
Three-dimensional archery tournaments are a good way to practice your hunting skills, because they take place in hunting environments.

Three-dimensional archery courses of all sizes are popping up all over the country as more and more archers are discovering the enjoyment of roaming the woods and fields shooting at bears, big cats, small game, and even the occasional African big-game animal. The benefits of shooting at life-size foam recreations of real game animals in an outdoor setting are obvious. Just keep in mind that the scoring rings on most 3-D targets are seldom in anatomically correct locations.

Another popular new shooting challenge is the Dart target system. To use this system, the shooter stands in a room with a large screen at the other end. A projector displays live-action footage of various big-game animals onto the special screen, and the archer shoots at the animal with an arrow that has a special blunt tip attached. Once the arrow hits the screen, the footage freezes, and the spot where the arrow impacted is shown, along with the point score for the shot. Some systems even tell you if you made a poor shooting choice. For the instinctive shooter, this provides little more than entertainment, as every shot is taken from the same distance. The only thing that changes from shot to shot is the animal and the size of the kill zone. But if you're looking for entertainment with minimal benefits, give the Dart system a try on some rainy day when it's too nasty to shoot outside.

RESPONSIBLE BOW HUNTING

The excitement and adrenaline rush at the approach of a game animal is part of the enjoyment of the hunt. I don't think any hunter ever has been, or ever will be, fully able to control his or her excitement at that moment. There is, however, one factor every hunter has complete and total control over: the decision whether or not to release the arrow. With the age-old art of hunting coming under fire from all directions in this day and age, we cannot afford to take irresponsible shots. Antihunters get their ammunition from stories and pictures of deer injured by hunters who, either through poor shot selection or by accident, wounded a deer that was seen by the general public. Please, only take shots at game animals that you know you can make. While every hunter, if he hunts long enough, makes a less-than-perfect shot on an animal and fails to recover it, this is the exception, not the norm.

As an ethical hunter, no amount of prestige or peer pressure should ever make you take a shot at game that you aren't sure you can make.

That's why it's important to practice shots that you might encounter in a hunting situation. Shot opportunities on game animals, especially those with long beards and big antlers, don't come along very often. Be prepared for them when they do by practicing and taking only shots that you are comfortable with.

- 8 -

Custom Bows

At some point in your archery career, you may want to purchase a custom bow. While bows made by companies like Bear and Martin are outstanding values and good shooters, they are still more or less mass-produced. In other words, the bow is built before it is needed. There's nothing wrong with that, and it doesn't mean the quality will be poor. But there's something special about talking to a custom bowmaker on the phone, telling him or her what your needs and wants in a bow are, and having that bowmaker say, "Yeah, I can build one like that for you."

Custom bowmakers, known as bowyers, are popping up right and left with the renewed interest in traditional archery. That's a good thing, because some of these new bowmakers have brought innovative ideas to the profession, resulting in better quality and performance.

A custom bow will not be cheap. There are several good reasons for the high price. First, the very word "custom" implies that it is specifically made for someone. There may also be exotic woods involved, which the bowyer must locate and purchase himself. The fact that all the work is done by hand, by very few people, means that a lot of pride and attention go into the bow. All in all, a good bowyer deserves his or her asking price.

But you shouldn't have to buy a pig in a poke, either. Most custom bowmakers have a color catalog they send to prospective customers. Look through the pages of *Traditional Bowhunter* magazine, the only magazine dedicated to traditional archery. Dozens of custom bowmakers are listed in its pages. Call or write for brochures from those bowyers

Traditional Bowhunter *magazine is devoted strictly to traditional archery and is an excellent source for information on bows and supplies as well as valuable tips on hunting and shooting with the traditional bow.*

that interest you. There is occasionally a small fee for the brochure. Once you've narrowed down your choices, call each bowyer and talk to him or her personally. Ask questions about the warranty. Ask about the options available. Find out how many bows a bowyer has made and how many have been returned for failures in workmanship. You're the one paying the money, so find out as much as you can about the bowyers and their products.

The best possible scenario is for you to find someone close by who owns a bow made by the bowyer you're interested in. At 3-D shoots, walk around and look at the custom bows being shot by the competitors. Attend outdoor sports shows, archery shows, and other gatherings that involve traditional archery. See if the owners of custom bows will let you handle their bows and look at them closely. Look down the edges of the limbs. Are they sanded smooth, or can you feel rough grain when you run your finger down the edge? Do you see any file marks or sanding marks? Are there any runs in the finish? Ask the owner's opinion of the bow and whether he or she would purchase another bow from that bowyer. In short, do your homework before investing a large sum of money in a custom bow that you may not like when you get it.

The listing of custom bowyers in appendix B is by no means even the tip of the iceberg. I've only included ones that I or someone I know has had experience with. Black Widow Custom Bows has a "test-drive" program where they'll send you the bow of your choice (you pay for it first, of course) and let you shoot it for one week. At the end of the week, you send the bow back. If it's returned undamaged, they'll either refund your money or apply it to the bow of your choice. To my knowledge, Black Widow is currently the only custom bow company that has this program. I've also shot bows made by Dave Johnson of Thunderbird Archery. Dave builds beautiful handmade longbows and flatbows from some awesome exotic and native hardwoods, and the bows perform as great as they look.

Whatever custom bowyer you choose, don't settle for anything less than exactly what you want. A custom bow is an investment and should last you for many years.

APPENDIX A

Traditional Archery Suppliers

Most archery shops in my area don't cater too much to the traditional archer, and I suspect a lot of readers of this book may face the same situation. The traditional archery suppliers listed here have a reputation for service and dependability, as well as having a lot of items that are hard to find. Some of these suppliers have web pages that at least have a partial catalog to look through, and occasionally they have special deals available only on their web page.

Alaska Bowhunting Supply
14000 Goldenview Dr.
Anchorage, AK 99516
(907) 345-4252
www.alaskabowhunting.com

The Footed Shaft
5510 North Highway 63
Rochester, MN 55906
(507) 288-7581
footedshaft@uswest.net

FS Discount Arrows & Supplies
2852 Walnut, Unit A2
Tustin, CA 92680
(800) 824-8261
www.fsdiscountarchery.com

Kustom King Traditional Archery
P.O. Box 11648
Merrillville, IN 46411
(219) 322-0790
www.kustom-king.com

Lost Nation Archery Supplies
26393 Mintdale
Sturgis, MI 49091
(888) 800-7880
www.bowsite.org/lostnation

Raptor Archery, Inc.
923 11th St.
Hood River, OR 97031
(541) 386-4503
www.raptorarchery.com

Three Rivers Traditional Archery
P.O. Box 517
Ashley, IN 46705
(260) 587-9501
www.3riversarchery.com

Valley Traditional Archery
  Supply
3814 Blair Rd.
Whitewater, CO 81527
(970) 243-8144
www.valleytradarchery.com

Wildcat Canyon Traditional
  Archery
1031 County Road 141
Durango, CO 81301
(970) 247-2894
beens@frontier.net

WinterRidge Archery
301 N.E. Hillcrest Dr.
Grant's Pass, OR 97526
(541) 476-6247
www.winterridgearchery.com

APPENDIX B

Custom Bowmakers

The following custom bowmakers all have years of experience and produce a fine-quality bow that is beautiful to look at. I highly recommend all of them. This is by no means a complete list. The Internet is the best place to do a search for custom bowmakers. Many bowyers have websites that display their bows and give detailed descriptions. Just type in the search word "traditional" and see how many returns you get.

Black Widow Custom Bows, Inc.
1201 Eaglecrest
P.O. Box 2100
Nixa, MO 65714
(417) 725-3113
www.blackwidowbows.com

Blacktail Bows
1655 Decker Pt. Rd.
Reedsport, OR 97467
(541) 271-2585
www.blacktailbows.com

Brackenbury Custom Bows
7305 W. Ridgecrest Ave.
Nine Mile Falls, WA 99026
www.brackenburybows.com

Fox Archery
701 W. Hwy 82
Wallowa, OR 97885
www.foxarchery.com

Great Northern Bowhunting
    Company
201 N. Main St.
P.O. Box 777
Nashville, MI 49073
www.mvcc.com/bu/gnbco

Hummingbird Custom Bows
9631 Vineyard Rd.
Mt. Pleasant, NC 28124
(704) 436-2509
www.hummingbirdbows.com

Pronghorn Custom Bows
2491 W. 42nd St.
Casper, WY 82604
pronghornbows@attbi.com

Robertson Stykbow
HCR 488 Box 7
Forest Grove, MT 59441
(406) 538-2818
www.robertsonstykbow.com

Sovereign Archery
P.O. Box 350
Datil, NM 87821
www.stickbow.com/sovereign-
  archery

Stotler Archery
P.O. Box 641
Rathdrum, ID 83858
(208) 687-0571
www.stotlerarchery.com

Thunderbird Traditional Archery
1090 G Street N.E.
Linton, IN 47441
(812) 847-1995
www.archery.at/thunderbird

TimberHawk Bows, Inc.
7895 State Road 446
Bloomington, IN 47401
(812) 837-9340
www.kiva.net/~thawk

Wapiti Custom Bows
490 S. Queen St.
Lakewood, CO 80266
members.aol.com/jkchastain

APPENDIX C

Resources

Over the years, I've grown to enjoy outdoor books and videos, particularly the ones that focus on traditional archery and bowhunting. I've compiled a list of my favorites, all of which are both educational and entertaining. They are listed in no particular order. I've placed an asterisk beside the ones that contain valuable tips and techniques.

Three Rivers Traditional Archery (see appendix A) has a large selection of videos and books, as well as reprints of some old classics. Black Widow Custom Bows (appendix B) has a good selection as well, including the videos listed below. I've read or watched all of these resources numerous times and never get tired of them.

BOOKS AND MAGAZINES

Become the Arrow, by Byron Ferguson. In his book, ESPN's Ferguson explains his method of shooting "barebow" and gives some tips on tuning. Available from Target Communications, 7626 W. Donges Bay Rd., Mequon, WI 53097, telephone (800) 324-3337. The price is about $13.

Howard Hill: The Man and the Legend, by Craig Ekin. This is a book about the man many consider to have been the greatest archer that ever lived. Biographical in nature, it covers Hill's life, adventures, and his part in the filming of the movie *Robin Hood*. ISBN 0937752-02-9.

Traditional Archery, by Sam Fadala. This book is a view into the world of traditional archery through the eyes of the author. It contains much valuable information, including a chapter on the famous Otzi, the 5,300-year-old hunter discovered frozen in the Italian Alps. ISBN 0-8117-2943-5. Available from Stackpole Books, 5067 Ritter Rd., Mechanicsburg, PA 17055, www.stackpolebooks.com.

Ishi in Two Worlds, by Theodora Kroeber. This book is about the last wild Indian known to have existed in North America. Ishi taught Dr. Saxton Pope the art of making bows. ISBN 0-520-00674-7.

Fred Bear's Field Notes: The Adventures of Fred Bear. Read about Fred's adventures as he stalks grizzly bears, moose, caribou, and many other animals with his trusty recurve bow. From Alaska to India, Fred and his companions enjoy traditional bowhunting at its finest. This is one you definitely want to read. ISBN 0-9619480-0-0.

The Archer's Bible, by Fred Bear. An interesting look at archery as it was at the time the book was written, in 1968. ISBN 0-385-08312-2.

In Defense of Hunting, by James A. Swan. Written about hunting by a hunter. Swan gives a valid defense of the sport and art of hunting. This book is good ammunition against antihunting. ISBN 0-06-251029-0.

*Traditional Bowhunter magazine. This valuable and entertaining resource features stories and articles written by well-known traditional bowhunters. For subscription information, contact: *Traditional Bowhunter,* 280 North Latah, Boise, ID 83706, telephone (208) 383-9019.

VIDEOS

*Selecting the Right Traditional Bow for You (and How to Get the Most out of It). If you're having a problem choosing a bow, this video will help.

*How to Shoot Instinctively Better than Ever. This video features Dan Bertalan and Denny Sturgis, Jr., in a variety of hunting situations. They also offer valuable tips on traditional bows and hunting.

*High Adventure Bowhunting. Wade Nolan and Dan Bertalan go on a series of hunts. Dan shares tips on traditional archery and bowhunting.

*Xtreme Bowhunting. Black Widow Custom Bows owner Ken Beck is joined by others for a series of hunts.

Tembo. A docudrama featuring Howard Hill on his African hunt. An old movie, but entertaining. Available from Stoney Wolf Productions, P.O. Box 459, Lolo, MT 59847, telephone (406) 273-0060. Stoney Wolf Productions has also produced numerous other videos, some of them featuring names like Mike Lapinski and Gene and Barry Wensel. Call for a list of videos.

The Sacred Hunt II. A film by Randall Eaton featuring music by Ted Nugent. Hunting is depicted as a traditional and proper way to bring young people into adulthood. This video was given high marks by some serious outdoorsmen. Available from The Sacred Hunt, P.O. Box 490, Ashland, OR 97520, telephone (877) SACRED-1.

APPENDIX D

Notes

Use this page to record important information on your draw length and your equipment. This page may be photocopied as needed.

Draw length: _____

Draw weight of bow at your draw length:_____

Arrow length: _____

Arrow size: _____

Field point or broadhead weight: _____

Brace height: _____

Nock point: _____

Miscellaneous information: _____

Index